We Use COUPONS, You Should Too!

How Coupons Changed My Life...

NATHAN "MR. COUPON" ENGELS

Ellechor Publishing House, LLC

www.ellechorpublishing.com

Table of Contents

Chapter One
The Power of a Piece of Paper

Let me tell you something about coupons....they are amazing little slips of nothing that have more power than you could possibly begin to either imagine or believe! They have the power to reinvent your finances. They have the power to feed your family and ease your mind. They have the power to **change your life.**

Don't believe me?

You're not alone. See, most people look at coupons and think they are nothing. That they are not worth the time, not worth the effort and not even worth the tiny drip of money they can manage to trickle off your grocery bill. But me? I look at those little slips of paper as life changing. Even life **saving** in some cases!

I'm a pretty simple guy. I like what I like and I tend to be a creature of habit that sticks to his routines day after day. I don't change quickly and I don't impress easily. I know this and I'm okay with it. But even I am constantly amazed at what those little slips of paper have done in my life.

But I'm getting ahead of myself. If you want to understand my perspective, you first need to understand where I'm coming from and from where I started.

MY STORY

I met my very first coupon in 2007. It wasn't a chance meeting either; it was a meeting of necessity. My finances were in shambles, with over $80,000 of debt, not including the house. I was in trouble, and I knew that something needed to change. But it was more than just a lifestyle change or implementing a new budget that I would discard in a matter of months; it was about changing the way I looked at money in its entirety.

Those tiny little pieces of paper known as coupons became my tool to do just that. They radically changed not only the way I looked at money, but also gave me a better understanding of the value of the products I was buying.

Why the big change? Well, I had this "Ah ha!" moment of sorts, one that struck me all at once and literally set my life onto a different path a few months into my coupon journey. Here's the deal:

Why would I pay for something later that I can get for free or cheap today?

Now, let that sink in a moment and really latch onto it. This is the basis of my life change, and this is the basis of everything else we are going to cover in this book. You have to understand that a coupon is a tool, one that can be used to effectively, even drastically, lower your grocery budget. But first you have to know how to use them, how to go beyond your grandmother's couponing, and really make this system, and this strategy, work for you and your family.

A CHANGE IN MINDSET

Let's start by talking about mindset. Most people walk into the grocery store with tunnel vision. They are focused on one thing and one thing only: this week. Their idea of a successful grocery trip is to make it through the next seven days before they trudge back through the door to try it all again. It's about survival. And, if they manage to save a buck or two on a sale item, then they tack a few bonus points onto their score. If it's a good sale, then they may buy a little extra, but their vision is blocked by that strict one-week timeframe.

So in order for you to really "get" this couponing thing and radically change your financial situation, you have to do one thing, right now: **you have to change your mindset and throw that one week timeframe completely out the window!** It hinders you

coupons changed my life. ARE YOU READY to change yours?

and blocks you to the possibilities of not just couponing, but of shopping smart at its most basic point. So do it. Right now. Vow to change the way you shop **forever!**

If I were to go back in time and coupon with my grandma, we could save some cash, sure. Our bill would be lower than the average shopper on any given week and it would be a good start. But as far as I'm concerned it would be just the beginning. Why? Because of the phrase you're about to hear....

Extreme couponing. You've all heard the term, and I am willing and even proud to wear that title when I walk into the store.

Why? Because I have used my "extreme couponing" to take those savings of just a few dollars and turn them into **thousands** every year.

We're back to that lifestyle change I was talking about.

When I set out to reinvent my finances and my lifestyle, I did just that. And the whole process started by changing my mindset. Today people see me walking through the store pushing a cart piled with 10 tubes of toothpaste or 20 packets of tuna, and they are stunned. I can see it all over their faces as they freeze mid-step with their own cart and wonder, "What in the world is that man going to do with all of that?!" Yep, I bet you're even guilty of having that thought yourself while reading this!

What am I going to do with all of that stuff? Well, let me show you how extreme couponing works.

WHAT IS EXTREME COUPONING?

We'll start with the toothpaste. I know that my family goes through an average of 20 tubes of toothpaste each year. Believe it or not, I have done the math on this and that number is right on track. Now, toothpaste is not something that we are going to get sick of, or suddenly stop using, it's more of an everyday staple. In short, unless we add more members to our family, we are going to go through about 20 tubes of toothpaste this year, no matter what. There are many items in our household just like toothpaste: toilet paper, shampoo, deodorant…I could go on and on and on.

AVERAGE YEARLY CONSUMPTION: 20 TUBES
Total Cost Per Year: $50
My Cost: $0

Today, when I throw those 10 tubes into my cart, they are absolutely free with the coupons in my hand. **Free**. As in I don't pay for them. Or, to put it another way, the coupons actually **pay** for the toothpaste. 100%. You'll still have to pay the tax in most states, but that's it. Just fork over Uncle Sam's share and you get to walk out with your goodies free and clear.

Here's how that transaction would look. I put my toothpaste up on the belt for the cashier to scan. They give me a total. I hand over my coupons and the cashier scans each one. When we are all done, I might owe a few cents in cash, but they pretty much tell me to have a nice day as I walk out the door with my free year's supply.

The tuna story happens to be true as well. When I bought 20 packets of tuna, my coupons were literally paying me to take them off of the shelves. I made money for each one that I threw in my cart, money that could be used to pay for other items on my shopping list. That's called an overage, and we will dive deeper into techniques like this later.

Sound too good to be true? It's not. It's legal, it's amazing and it's something that you can do, too.

YEAR-LONG SHOPPING

Am I hoarding toothpaste? Am I trying to single-handedly corner the market on tuna? Not in the least. I'm shopping *smart*. I'm purchasing something I will use, stocking up on that item, and effectively taking it off of my grocery list for the rest of the year.

But, you might ask, *why* is it important to take items off your grocery list for a year?

To answer that, think about how the average American family approaches their weekly trip to the grocery store. They start with a list of items, like toothpaste and tuna, which their family will use in a given week. Once they get to the store, they buy the items on their list...**regardless of price.**

Why? Because they need those items. That is what their family uses and what they need to get through the next week. Imagine a different way to shop. Imagine instead of running to the store every time you need something, you simply walk down to your pantry. Read this sentence carefully: I'm buying something I need when I **don't** need it. It's the heart of that mindset change I mentioned earlier: Why pay for something later when it's free or cheap today? i.e. the toothpaste is off my list and that money is back in my budget. This concept is central to couponing successfully. We get into strategic stockpiling later in the book, so stay tuned. Basically the key point is this:

QUIT GOING TO THE STORE WITH A GIANT GROCERY LIST!

Me? I go to the store each week with a list of about 5 to 10 items. They are the core essentials and the key items that I am looking for in a given week. Sometimes it's toilet paper, sometimes its frozen vegetables, the item doesn't really matter. What matters is that I am going to stock up on these items while I can get them at their rock bottom price. That price may be extremely cheap, it may be free and it may even involve the store paying me to take the item off of their hands for them. Yep, that happens too!

Stocking up on these items, like toilet paper, means that it is now marked off of my list for the year. Now I don't have to pay for it week after week. This is why I don't spend hundreds of dollars every week at the grocery store. My list is small – ironic for an extreme couponer, right? I buy lots of an item when the price is low (locking in my very low price), and the result is the removal of that item from my list. Why would I need to buy more soap if I already have 20 bars? Speaking of soap, when was the last time you bought some? Do you remember how much you paid for it? I know exactly how much I paid…nothing. Not a single cent. I don't have to pay for soap anymore, because unlike the majority of the country, when I find that great sale I stock up and buy enough to last me for a long, long time.

Here is an example of what my average weekly grocery list looks like. (See picture)

That's it! That's what I'm after and that's the extent of what I am interested in when I walk through the door.

Why does this work? It works because the bulk items are different from week to week. While one week you may find me stocking up on toilet paper and frozen veggies, the next could be almonds and yogurt. Every single week is different, and each one works to replenish something different in my pantry.

Nathan's GROCERY LIST
- Milk
- Fresh Fruit/Veggies
- Eggs
- Meat
- 5 to 10 bulk items

So there it is. That's the big secret that can literally save you thousands of dollars each and every year.

WHERE TO START

You're doing it right now. Reading! That is the hands down best advice that I can give you.

For starters, read this book. Then go check out our website at WeUseCoupons.com where you will find literally hundreds of articles and videos, each one offering a different tidbit of wisdom for you to absorb. WeUseCoupons is a coupon community where thousands of people go to find support when they start couponing!

I'm not telling you to do anything different than what I have done myself. When I first started couponing, there were very few websites out there. I found a few that explained what to do, where to go and how this complex savings game worked. I remember when I first tried to test the waters of couponing. I was like a sponge! I wanted to figure it all out and I wanted to do it now. Right now!

But it takes time.

My garage didn't start out with thousands of items packed onto every available space…it started with 7. I remember this day like it was yesterday. I walked into a store, used my coupons and walked out with 7 bottles of shampoo for $2 total. I kept thinking to myself that I was losing my mind. I mean who in the world goes out and buys 7 bottles of shampoo when they don't need it?

Today I realized that it was the start of something big. For one thing, I haven't had to pay for shampoo now in going on 4 years. Every time I catch it on sale and I have a coupon, I buy it and pay nothing! This system is designed to empower **you** and you won't believe how well it works; my shampoo example alone shows me that it works!

AN ADDED BENEFIT

Here's another reason to consider giving couponing a try. It gives you the opportunity to help those that you love in their time of need. Imagine facing your friends, neighbors or loved ones after the loss of a job. They're hurting, truly hurting and looking for help.

Could you make a difference in their lives? Could you offer them anything other than comforting words?

My wife and I, we don't earn a lot of money. For us, it would be a huge sacrifice to give someone $50 week after week. But ask me to give them $200 worth of groceries and I could do it over and over again. That is the power of coupons!

Since we started couponing not only have we gained control over our finances, but we have also extended our vision to reach out to those in need. This year, my personal giving goal is something I never would have even dreamed about in the past. This year, my wife and I are going to attempt to give away more than we made last year.

NOW THAT'S A STRANGE CONCEPT!

We want to give back to our community and we are going to do so in the best way that we know how. We may not be able to give away thousands of physical dollars, but we have tens of thousands of dollars in product that we can use to make a difference. That's tens of thousands of dollars that are going to change lives and to helping those who need it most.

That is **the** power you can find in those little pieces of paper. Little slips that have long been overlooked now have the power to change your life, your community and most of all, the way you shop!

READY TO GO?

I want you to use this book as a tool, one that will help you as you begin to shape your own shopping habits and come up with the perfect couponing plan for your family. I'll show you the basics, and even the not so basics, but how you make it work is up to you. We are going to cover the idea of stockpiling, look at how grocery stores think and even get back to basics with a section on Couponing: 101.

In short, everything that you need will be ready and waiting for you by the time we are done. So let's get started by looking at some couponing myths and misconceptions that people, maybe even you, have about using coupons.

Chapter Two
Common Couponing Myths & Misconceptions

Have you ever caught yourself saying that coupons are a waste of time? That the pennies they save don't make up for the time it takes you to cut them out? Or, maybe you've said that using coupons is too complicated and that you can never find deals on the products you actually use? If this sounds familiar, than I can promise you you're not alone. In fact, the couponing world is full of these types of myths and misconceptions.

We've all heard them. We all know they are out there. So before we go any further we need to take just a few minutes to clear the air on all these common misconceptions about coupons that float through both your mind and your conversations on a daily basis.

Trust me, I've heard it all and it makes me sad. It truly saddens my heart that people have deluded themselves into literally opening up the trash can and dumping their hard-earned cash into its gaping black abyss.

The reality about couponing is that if I can do it…anyone can. I am not a rocket scientist. I don't have some kind of crazy advanced degree that marks me as an aerospace engineer. I have simply developed a system that works for me, and now I want to share it with you.

Remember this. Like anything else in life, **coupons are what you make them to be**. You may dislike them. You may even hate them, but I know for a fact that every single one of you would prefer to have a fatter wallet and fuller cabinets. I honestly haven't met the person yet who would want to pay **more** for the items they use each and every day.

Misconceptions are everywhere. Every part of couponing is packed with them from the time it takes to clip them to how you can use them once you do. I will be the first to admit that I once shared many of these misconceptions. I'll go ahead and admit it: "Hello, my name is Nathan, and I used to throw my coupons away with everyone else."

Today I have learned that once you know how to coupon the right way, many of these myths become laughable. But the only way to counteract their negative influence is to address the issue head on. Once we have, I hope that you will see that couponing is not impossible; that it is something you **can** do and you can do it with ease!

Myth 1: I DON'T HAVE THE TIME TO CLIP COUPONS AND FIND DEALS

This is the big one. It is the most common objection out there and the one that I find myself coming up against time and time again.

And, truthfully, I understand.

Over the years the majority of us have been trained to ignore coupons because we have been told they are not necessary for frugal shopping. If they are not necessary, then it must be a waste of time to seek them out and use them.

"Why should we make time for something that is not necessary?"

Sound familiar? Yep, it does to me, too.

Here's the deal. There is the rare person out there who actually does not have the time to coupon. They truly don't. And I will be the first to admit that couponing is not for everyone. But, I will also say that the **majority** of people who make this excuse may simply not be managing their time well.

Time management is an important aspect to becoming a successful couponer. Regardless of the couponing system that you use, this process does take time and it does take dedication. It is something that you have to stay on top of week after week as you search out the good deals and find those rock bottom prices you are searching for. Then when you have your system down pat, you might change it to meet the needs of new time constraints in your life. Systems can and will change throughout your new lifestyle with couponing.

Couponing, in truth, is not for everyone and it is not always easy. I can't sit here and promise you that you can dedicate five minutes a week to the task and walk away saving hundreds of dollars. But I am going to show you how to simplify the process with my own proven strategies; strategies that will work to save you both time and money. I save thousands of dollars every year and haven't paid for dish soap, toothpaste or shampoo in years.

I hope that is enough to make a believer out of you!

In terms of time, I spend about five hours a week organizing, clipping and shopping. Some people tend to spend more, others spend less, but at the end of the day it all comes down to the system that you use. Also, keep in mind that multi-tasking is a crucial skill for any dedicated couponer. One tip that works for me involves a shopping list. Each week I put together a detailed list for my trip that organizes both the items that I need as well as the coupons that I will use. This saves me time at the store and greatly shortens the overall process. Also, once you learn how to coupon my way, your pantry will become quite full. This means that you will have fewer items on your list each week and be able to go to the store even less often.

In the end it all comes down to this: If something is important to you, then you will make time for it. I make time for family, I make time for work, I make time for fun and I make time for saving money. If saving money is a top priority for you, then clipping coupons should find its way to the top of your list. Here's the deal: I work hard for my money. And, because I work hard for my money, I'm also willing to work hard at saving that money. Even if it takes me a little time to do it.

Myth 2: COUPONS SIMPLY AREN'T WORTH IT

The first time I heard this particular objection I was smack in the middle of teaching a couponing class. Thinking quickly I pulled out my wallet and dropped a dollar bill on the floor. Then looking at the class I asked whether or not I should pick it up. They all kind of laughed as they shouted, "Of course!" Smiling right along with them I next asked if any of them would actually walk by and NOT pick it up. More laughter and no hands went into the air. Everyone was willing to pick up my dollar for me.

But when I reached into my binder and dropped a popular coupon on the floor I got a very different response. This time when I asked who would pick it up, only a few people raised their hands.

Bending down I picked up my coupon and held it so the class could see what it was for. I explained that the coupon in question was for one free box of $3 popcorn. It was actually worth far more than the dollar I had dropped before.

Coupons are literally one small step from currency. They are waiting to be used **by you,** and when used in the right way they are one of the best ways out there to keep more of your money safe and secure in your own pocket.

They are more than just worth it, they are amazingly effective!

To me a coupon is like cash. If I see one in a parking lot, I pick it up. If I see one in a store, I grab it. I may use it, I may not but if I don't take the time to at least pick the thing up then I'm not going to get the chance to find out.

At one point I did a personal experiment in order to figure out how much time I spend versus how much money I saved. During the week of the experiment, I spent two and half hours couponing, clipping and searching for deals. I then spent two and half hours going to the three different grocery stores. So I spent a total of five hours saving money that week.

After looking at my receipts I saved $227 that week and spent $39 in cash. So I made a "wage" of $45 dollars an hour! I don't know about you, but to me that is quite a happy number!

Look at it this way. Outside of your mortgage or your rent, groceries are generally the biggest household expense. If you could save 60-70% on your mortgage every month you would do it in a heartbeat. So why wouldn't you do the same on your groceries? Coupons are worth it. You just have to know how to use them.

Myth 3: COUPONS ARE TOO COMPLICATED

Yet another old favorite! I can't tell you how many times I have heard a variation of this sentence. "This seems so complicated just to save a few bucks on your grocery bill."

Hmmm…let's look at that statement.

First off, food prices are going up. In some cases they are going up considerably. Yet, no matter how high the price goes, we all have to eat. We have to feed our families, we have to feed our kids and we have to feed ourselves. As far as I see, that is not going to change. The only thing that can change is the price, and it rarely goes down.

How can you affect the price? With coupons. Can they be complicated? Absolutely! But complicated does not mean impossible. It just means that you have to take the time to learn about the process of couponing and how you can use that process to your advantage.

Plus, you aren't in this alone. On my website, WeUseCoupons. com, you will find literally thousands of couponers who have been where you are and they are willing to help. They have the answers to your questions; all you have to do is ask.

Besides, if you are holding this book in your hands, then you're already halfway there. The details can feel overwhelming, but I encourage you to stick with it. Like anything else in life there is a learning curve with couponing. In fact, couponing is very much like a game of chess. There are lots of different pieces to the game and no one learns how to play it over night. But take heart, it won't be long until you begin to see patterns and trends in the madness. You will begin to build your system and get comfortable in your routine as the savings mount and your pantry fills. Then, before you know it, someone else will be stopping *you* in the store to ask you a coupon question of their own.

Myth 4: COUPONS ARE FOR JUNK, NOT FOR PRODUCTS I USE

I'll be the first to admit, I don't use the occasional cookie coupon because I can't have them in the house. Even if they are free! I know myself, and know that I won't be able to resist the temptation! I like to think that I have a well balanced diet, and for the most part coupons are a big part of that.

What constitutes a well-balanced couponing diet?

For starters, my family enjoys a bag of flash frozen veggies every night since I was able to get those for $0.10 each. I bought dozens of them at that price and we have been eating them ever since. How about bagged salads? Or juice? Or protein bars? Or veggie burgers? Or water filters? All of these items have coupons and all of them can be found at a fraction of the regular retail price.

But that is just the beginning! You have to realize that as manufacturers become more and more health conscious they are going to offer more coupons for those healthy items we all crave.

Plus, even if you are not one for processed foods, you still have to keep your house clean. You have to keep up with your personal hygiene as you wash your clothes and dishes. Everyone has a bathroom in their house and bathrooms always need toilet paper; it doesn't matter if you are the president or a pauper!

The great part is that all of these items usually have coupons floating around. Coupons are not limited to groceries! As I've said, I personally never pay for toothpaste and I pay pennies for detergent or deodorant. I can find hand soap for next to nothing and have enough band aids to wrap myself up like a mummy next Halloween. These items, even though they are not groceries, fall into your grocery budget. They are the items that your household uses from week to week and they are items that you have to replenish.

Having a healthy diet is great, and it is something that we all strive for. Here is my challenge. Take the time to really learn about couponing and the offers that are available. I think that you will be surprised at the balanced diet that you can offer your family at a fraction of the cost you are used to spending. Even when that diet just happens to include a bit of Edy's Ice Cream that you scored for free! Healthy eating and couponing go together. It's about choices and I choose to save money!

Myth 5: GENERIC ITEMS ARE ALWAYS CHEAPER

Does this not just make you cringe? I literally shudder every single time I hear this slip from someone's mouth.

First off, I try to stay away from words like "always" and "never." They just open you up for being wrong and having to take a big ol' bite of your own foot. Secondly, just because this principle has been shoved down our throats by the so-called financial experts doesn't make it true. It's just something that most of us have swallowed because we have heard it 5,000 times.

Now, I will preface this section with this. If you are not a coupon shopper then generic items are often cheaper. They are also often of lower quality and, in my opinion, poorer taste. (Have you tried generic oatmeal? Yuck.)

But if you use coupons it is rare that you will find a better deal on a generic option! Don't believe me? Let me give you a few examples:

A few recent purchases and what I would have spent:

Value Size Package 4oz	Regular Package 2oz	Small Package 1oz
Price: $3.49	Price: $1.99	Price: $1.19
Coupon: -$1	Coupon: -$1 (two coupons allowed)	Coupon: -$1 four coupons allowed)
Unit Cost: $2.49	Unit Cost: $.99	Unit Cost: $.19
Final Cost for 4oz: $2.49	Final Cost for 4oz: $1.98	Final Cost for 4oz: $.76

Now any good couponer will tell you that there is a time and place for generic items. I buy generic when I don't have a coupon for an item, or if I have a coupon for an item and the generic is cheaper. The latter is rare, but can happen. It simply means that the manufacturer isn't very motivated in selling their product!

Trust me my friends, it's all about the timing.

I often say that I eat better on coupons, and get more name brand items that I ever did without them. You can see the price differences on items we all buy almost every month. Generics can be cheaper, but not generally. Using coupons the right way will beat the generic's price and get you a better quality product for less!

Myth 6: POOR PEOPLE USE COUPONS, AND I'M NOT POOR

If this is the reason you aren't using coupons, then you've been had. A recent survey by NCH Marketing Services revealed that 75 percent of consumers in all income brackets use coupons sometimes and the highest rate of coupon clippers have an income of $25,000 - $50,000. I happen to fall in that income range myself, and I don't consider myself to be poor. Also according to NCH (an international coupon processor), three out of four shoppers use coupons at some point while shopping for groceries.

In truth, back when I started using coupons, I really did need help, but I was embarrassed to admit it. It felt like by using coupons, I was sending a message to everyone in the store that I was unable to afford groceries. I quickly found out that not only was that not the case, but other customers in line with me idolized my savings. They wished they could duplicate my checkouts!

So what does this mean? It means first of all that those in the middle-income bracket are the most dedicated coupon users out there. It also means that just about everyone, regardless of income, uses a coupon at some point in his or her shopping travels. Basically we can use this data to understand that all people like saving money. Most people I know LOVE a deal; it's in our nature! It's not poor people that use coupons; it's smart people!

Myth 7: BUYING IN BULK AT WAREHOUSE STORES WILL ALWAYS BE CHEAPER

There's that "always" word again!

Here's the truth about the big warehouse stores. If you shop there week after week *AND* you use what you buy, i.e. you have an enormous family or a pack of teenage boys that consume everything in sight, then you will probably save money over the life of your membership. The question is, how much will you save? The reality is that most people don't save the money they think they do and many don't even save the cost of their membership.

Sad, but true!

While those big package stores might be tempting, they are also pricy. Plus, packing that product into one package means that you only get the chance to use a single coupon on what would be 12 or more separate items at your local grocery store. (To make matters worse most warehouse stores won't even let you use coupons) Most items in that big warehouse can be found at your local grocery store and I can almost promise that they will be on sale somewhere. Somewhere that the packages are smaller and where the coupon policy is much more user friendly. From diapers to deodorant, smaller packaged items can be found at cheaper prices (by unit) than the big warehouse stores.

For consumers that don't use coupons, please shop around! Warehouse stores have a great gimmick, but unfortunately that is all it is usually. They make you pay to save and they make you buy in extremely large quantities – quantities so large that often times the item will spoil or ruin before you can possibly hope to use it all. You may find a deal here or there, but it's rare to save enough to cover the membership fee.

ANNUAL COST OF WAREHOUSE MEMBERSHIP $49 in 2012

But don't take my word for it. Let's break it down with the math using the same Cheerios price I did for the generic example: A warehouse-sized box of Cheerios usually has about three bags inside one large box and costs somewhere between $5 and $6. At the grocery store I would pay $0.75 for those same three boxes! Huge difference!

Why would you pay the 'warehouse' price for something, when your local grocery store has the same exact item on sale for 75% less after coupons? Just because you like the bigger box and they charge you a membership fee?

I'm thinking not.

Marketing and packaging have convinced consumers and frugal shoppers alike that warehouse stores are the way to save. This is simply not true. On top of that, warehouse stores encourage you to buy things you would otherwise not purchase. Ever heard of sample day? Have you ever purchased something because you tried and liked it? The mentality of many warehouse shoppers is striking. Most assume a warehouse store is cheaper and therefore those consumers are much more likely to purchase MORE because, hey it's a good deal, right? Wrong. You may save 10%-15% off your bill, but by simply being an aware consumer, you can save much more at your local grocery store even if you leave the coupons at home.

Myth 8: IT'S NOT WORTH IT TO SHOP AT MULTIPLE STORES EACH WEEK

Some people hate to shop. I know you're out there and that the idea of going to multiple stores each week is about as appealing as raking your nails down an oversized chalkboard.

But would you still hate to shop if you were getting the items for free? Would you be able to stomach going to two, or even three, separate stores if you were able to keep the total under $10 at each one?

Kind of changes the perspective a bit!

No average shopper would go to more than one grocery store unless they had good reason. For me, saving hundreds of dollars each and every week is a very good reason! Different stores have different sales, and I have to be flexible if I want to be in a position to take advantage of those sales. This is where the big savings come from and I have to be open to that fact.

Do I do it every single week? Nope. But, if the sales are good then I am always willing!

Myth 9: PEOPLE WHO USE COUPONS BUY THINGS THEY WON'T USE

I don't waste money on things I won't use, but if it's free it can't hurt me to buy it! Part of building a new coupon mindset is understanding that simply because you have a coupon, doesn't mean you should or have to buy a product you wouldn't ever use.

Would you spend money on a size 3 shirt when you're a size 8? Of course not!

But what about this? Would you buy a size 3 shirt if it were **free**, even if you wore a size 8? Absolutely! Why? Because you can use it as a gift or you can donate that shirt to someone in need.

Using coupons for items that you plan to let sit on your shelf until they mold is foolish. So have a plan. If you run across a free item, one that you won't use but costs you nothing, find a way to use that item to help someone else. Pass on the savings and everybody wins!

When you learn the new way to coupon, you realize that there is a coupon for almost everything you use. You just have to have the patience and experience to know when and where to use them.

Myth 10: IT'S EMBARRASSING TO USE COUPONS!

I will be honest and say that there have been a few times when I wasn't comfortable hauling my coupon binder around in a store. I mean, it's this big clunky thing that you just have to plop out there for the world to see! Basically I was embarrassed and more than a little worried about what people might think.

That was then. Now? After years of doing this I realize that the majority of people out there understand what I am doing, and more, wish they could do it themselves. Sure, I run across the odd grump that has to throw in their two cents about my coupons usage, but the overall response has been positive.

But a funny thing tends to happen when I use coupons. People notice!

When I first started using coupons, I was extremely self-conscious, especially being a guy, thinking that coupons were for women. But people, my wife will tell you there is nothing sexier than a man with a coupon binder. I get more positive comments about my coupon binder than I care to admit! I also have the most wonderful experiences in line at the grocery store. Here's an example…

About six months ago, I was checking out at a major grocery store, and they were very busy. I was a little worried because people got behind me, and I probably had about 60 coupons to use that day. I told the lady behind me that it might be a while, but she told me not to worry. So the cashier rang up all the items, which came to around $85. Then she started scanning my coupons. The lady behind me starting getting vocal while she waited, but not negatively, as you might think; she was actually drawing attention to me and what I was doing, and even started to clap as my total got under ten dollars. Other cashiers in other lines started to watch, too, and finally I ended up paying $4.83. Customers came up to me after I finished and asked me how I did that, because it was amazing!

People are looking to save money, and what I've come to discover is that it's cool! Now when I go into that grocery store, cashiers INVITE me into their lines because they want to see what I'm doing so they can do it themselves.

CHEAP IS Chic Frugal IS FABULOUS

I'm not embarrassed anymore. I am proud to be a couponer and I am proud to show others how they can replicate my success.

So now you know the truth. We've pulled back the curtain and given you a glimpse into what couponing is really like without all the myths and misconceptions that tend to cloud the issue. Now, the next step is simple. It's time to learn how it's done. As we move into the next chapter we are going to start talking about more practical matters. A true Couponing: 101. I tell you this because I want you to be encouraged, to be empowered about what it to come and not be nervous or overwhelmed. I know you can do this, now I just have to convince you of that fact!

Chapter Three
Basic Couponing Techniques

Couponing can be tricky. I'm the first one to admit this fact and I often joke with people that the whole process is about as clear as mud.

I also tell them that it's not rocket science!

Truly the **process** is fairly easy, **but** it does take practice and it does take time. It also takes a good dose of experience to get things right each and every time. So with this chapter my goal is to try and help you take two huge steps forward as I share my experiences with you.

Think of it like Couponing 101! We are going to start at the beginning and work our way through the wonderful maze of the couponing world. I know that it might seem like a lot, but if you want to save money with coupons then first you have to know how to use them!

WHAT'S A COUPON?

Starting at the beginning means starting with the basics.

First, you need to know what a coupon is and its purpose. As in, why do manufactures and retailers print out these little beauties in the first place? They do so to promote their product. Coupons are promotional tools, ones that are presented to the general public in the form of a small document, i.e. the coupon itself. That document can then be redeemed for a discount on specific products.

Now, keep in mind that coupons are issued by both stores and manufacturers. And, while we will get into the difference between these types of coupons shortly, just know that each type has a specific purpose in terms of store or product promotion. However the one common denominator between all coupons is that they will feature a specific savings amount or other special offer designed to persuade you as the consumer *to make a purchase.*

The **traditional** mindset is that a coupon is a marketing tool that you should avoid. I mean, you can use one when you're buying something that you would any ways but overall the process isn't really worth your time.

My friends, **that** traditional mindset is wrong!

Yes, you do need to understand that a coupon is a marketing tool. But, in the right hands, they can also transform into a stack of cold hard cash that you can use to drastically reduce your grocery budget.

So why does a manufacturer or store issue a coupon in the first place? Well, they do it because they know that a crazy high percentage of those coupons will never be redeemed. To them a coupon is just a marketing tool; one that they use in the same way that they do a commercial, radio or print ad.

You see, with a commercial, the manufacturer must pay the television station up front. They pay several hundred thousand dollars and get 30 seconds of airtime. With coupons, the manufacturer still pays, they just pay later, when you actually redeem the coupon. They make a budget based on trends and how many coupons have been redeemed in the past.

Notice how the design of most coupons mirrors every other ad that you see for that same product? It's done on purpose.

Companies understand that the more you lay eyes on their product the more likely you are to remember it. The more you remember it, the more likely you are to buy it. I tell you this because I want you to understand the system. Knowledge is power and the more you know about marketing strategies, the more you can use those same strategies to your own advantage.

WHERE DO I FIND COUPONS?

Ah…..memories! Back when I first started couponing I can remember the mad Sunday morning rush that I would throw myself into each and every week. It went something like this: I would roll out of bed no later than 5am just to **run** to Wal-Mart and hope that the newspapers were already on the shelves. The earlier I got there, the earlier I could find deals. I knew the difference that couponing was making in my life and the life of my family and I couldn't wait to get started!

Trust me, it was intense!

In those days my couponing world was limited to the newspaper and the Internet. That's it! Now I know that coupons are absolutely everywhere. They are literally staring at you from right under your nose, and you just have to know where to look.

NEWSPAPERS

This is the biggie. First, and possibly the most obvious of the group, is your local newspaper. Most local Sunday papers come stocked with coupon booklets known as "inserts." If you have ever thumbed through a Sunday paper then you know exactly what I am talking about. And not just the Sunday paper: you should know that coupons can pop up any day of the week, especially if you live in rural areas.

Now, there are three **main** types of inserts to look for; Red Plum, SmartSource and P&G Saver. I say **main**, because occasionally you will come across something different, but these are the big 3.

Let's start with the P&G Saver. This insert comes out once a month and you will generally find it on the first Sunday of the month at hand. What you need to know about the P&G Saver is that it is only for Proctor & Gamble products (thus the P&G) and the coupons all expire within about 30 days. Just in time for you to get the next insert!

Many couponers look forward to the P&G Saver because it always has a few nice goodies inside. Great coupons make a variety of different items either free or very close to it. The coupons are similar from month to month, you'll always find things like Dawn dishwashing liquid, toilet paper, paper towels and toothpaste.

Next, let's talk about SmartSource. SmartSource, which is often abbreviated to SS in couponing shorthand, is distributed by News Corporation and is the most widely distributed coupon booklet in the US today. SmartSource can be found almost every single Sunday, except holidays, and on occasion you will find more than one SmartSource insert per week. And SmartSource is packed! This is often the most valuable insert of the week and is definitely the biggest in terms of the sheer number of coupons that you can expect in a given week.

Red Plum, or RP, rounds out our group and is distributed by Valassis Marketing. Like SmartSource, Red Plum is a weekly insert that can be found in most Sunday papers. However, in recent years Red Plum has started to move away from the standard distribution models in favor of a more direct approach. Many areas now find that their weekly Red Plum insert is delivered directly to their home.

Always remember that around the holidays coupons are often missing from your Sunday paper. Even coupons need time off! A good rule of thumb is to check the newspaper before buying it. There is nothing worse than to buy two papers, get home and there are no coupons inside! Another good tip to remember is to check coupon blogs and forums. On my site, we post something called a coupon preview which will alert you to the coupons inside the paper even before you buy it! If you're not sure about the whole scheduling thing, then just check in with me at WeUseCoupons.com every week!

SAVINGS TIP:

Check to See If Your Newspaper Has a Coupon Subscription. Some Newspapers Offer Discounts on Multiple Subscriptions as well

Before we move on, I want to add a quick note on frugality. The idea here is to save money, right? Well, one way to do that is to always find the best price for your Sunday paper. In most towns, the newspaper is generally more expensive on Sundays. Right, wrong, or indifferent, it just is. A way to get around this is to check out your local dollar stores. Many times dollar stores will offer the Sunday paper for a dollar and significantly cut down the price of what you would pay otherwise. You can also keep your eyes out for local grocery or drug stores to put the paper on sale. Yep, even the newspaper goes on sale!

THE INTERNET

The Internet is absolutely packed with coupons...as long as you know where to look. Manufacturer's websites, store websites, coupon websites, it is a never-ending list and learning to manage it can quickly feel overwhelming! So, to cut down on the clutter, I recommend that you focus your online couponing efforts to a few, key, **safe** websites.

- SmartSource.com
- RedPlum.com
- Coupons.com
- CouponNetwork.com

Each of these sites are extremely reputable and they offer a menu of coupons that boasts both breadth and depth. Keep in mind though that online couponing is not a free-for-all that throws open the floodgates of savings! There are rules to be followed and not doing so can land you in a heap of trouble.

Here's the deal. Each of the sites listed about will usually allow you to print 2 copies of any given coupon, the idea being that the first one is for you to use and the second is allowed in case of a printer error. Once you have printed your allotted amount you will receive a message that states something like, "Sorry, you have reached your print limit for this coupon."

At this point, if you really want to print more, then just go to another computer, as the limits are logged via that IP address of your machine, not by your name and not by your address.

Here is where people have been getting themselves into trouble. Once you reach your print limit on your spiffy 4-in-1 photo printer, it might be tempting to just flip those coupons up to the top and run off a few copies.

This, my friends, is a very bad idea! **And it is illegal**!

Why? Because each coupon that you print out has a unique code assigned to it that is tied to the computer that printed it. Therefore, if you copy that coupon, you can get caught. And the companies involved do not find this practice funny or acceptable. In fact, more and more manufacturers are becoming aggressive in searching for and prosecuting people who copy and then use online coupons. Also, because the fraud rates have gotten so high, many stores are now refusing to take Internet coupons, or severely limiting their usage, which just makes things harder for all of us.

So, simple rule of thumb, **never** copy or scan a coupon, even if you printed it off your computer. Just use the original and just be happy with what you have! It's not only about ethics but about what is legal and what isn't.

TEARPADS

Tearpads are these great little pads that hang on a shelf, rack or display. Usually they are in front of the product they relate to. You can find them in grocery stores, drug stores and even in convenience stores. In fact, I have found some great drink coupons in gas station convenience stores that I have never seen anywhere else!

The great thing about tearpads is that you can take a few. This does not however mean that you should take them all, of course! For me, if it is a good coupon then I will usually take a few and I always make sure to leave plenty behind for others. Remember, be kind and leave some behind!

Quick note about tearpads. Tearpads are often brought into a store by the vendors that deliver the product. For example, the Coke driver, the Pepsi driver, and the Lays chips driver. So, if you see these vendors in the store, you might (very politely!) ask if they have any coupons with them. The answer might be no, but if there is a marketing campaign going on, then it might be yes!

PEELIES/BLINKIES

Peelie – A peelie is a coupon that you peel off of an item when **you** buy it. If you don't buy the product, then it's not your coupon. Trust me, it is very frustrating to find a product on the shelf and see that shiny empty space where the peelie has already been snagged by someone who left the product behind. Some people won't agree with my stance on this, and I understand that, but the truth is that the manufacturer is offering that coupon as an incentive to buy that **specific** product. It's not a tearpad and we shouldn't treat it as such.

Blinkie – A blinkie is a machine that spits out coupons. These machines are usually situated right in front of the product in question. They are always found in grocery stores and they are always moving around the store from week to week. If I like the coupon in the blinkie, then I will usually stand there and let it spit out 5 or 6 until I move on.

Blinkie Machine

A side note: I have also noticed something recently. A few times I have walked off from a blinkie after pulling 2 coupons because once I pulled the second one, nothing else came out. I just assumed the machine was empty and moved on. Then, when I had to come back down the aisle because I forgot something I noticed a coupon sticking out. I grabbed two more and the same thing happened. It seems that some blinkies now come with a sensor that adds in a significant delay after 2 coupons are pulled back to back. This is most likely a way for companies to attempt to control the flow of the coupons and keep a few shoppers from emptying the machine. So just be patient, you obviously don't want to empty the machine, but if it's a good coupon, make sure to pick up a few to capitalize on the savings. Remember the machine might be empty…or it might just want you to **think** that it's empty!

CATALINAS

Catalinas are manufacturer coupons that print out during the check out process at some stores, specifically grocery stores. These offers are tied to the items that you purchase and can often be very high value.

- Common catalinas include:
- Specific amount of money off of your next order or purchase. (OYNO)
- High value coupons for specific items.
- Produce coupons.
- Other special offers, such as a free Shutterfly photo book.
- Register Rewards from Walgreens are also catalinas

Now, I want to take just a moment to clear up an issue that might be confusing for some of you. I know that it was confusing to me in the beginning! When we say "Catalina," we are talking about the company that puts out this type of coupon, Catalina Marketing. Some call these coupons "YourBucks." If you are poking around the Internet, then you will see them referred to either way, so don't let it trip you up. It's one of those times where the brand name has taken over for the item. Like how we are all prone to call a "tissue," a "Kleenex."

Right now you can see all current Catalina offers at CouponNetwork.com, and it seems like it will stay that way for a while. This is great because you can stop by any time, and see if there might be something wonderful that you want to add to your cart. It's also wise to register on CouponNetwork. They will send you updates about specific catalinas in your area.

SAMPLE DISPLAYS

Have you ever walked into a store and noticed that they are sampling products that day? Well, where there are samples there are usually coupons, very good coupons! So don't just breeze on by. Take a few minutes to stop by and see what they are talking about. You might just find a pretty fantastic coupon. Just make sure to ask the person attending the table if you can take a few extra coupons; most likely they will be more than happy to give you extras.

IN THE MAIL

It takes some time, but if you are willing to reach out and contact the manufacturers of the products that you buy, then you just might find yourself with some pretty fantastic coupons stuffing your mailbox. First, check out the back of the product you are interested in for a 1-800 number. Then, call and tell the company how good, or bad, their product happens to be. Ask them if they have any coupons and you might just be surprised at what they send out. Manufacturers are often eager to put these coupons in their customer's hands.

TIME SAVING TIP:

Google is Your Friend When Searching for Company Lists. Many Coupon Websites Will Also Have Lists of Companies You Can Contact for Coupons

TRADING COUPONS OR COUPON TRAINS

On WeUseCoupons.com you can join a coupon train and trade coupons with other members. We often have several members who are trading with each other by checking wish lists and making offers. This is one of the main reasons why you should always clip and save every single coupon. You never know what other people are looking for and your trash may be someone else's treasure. And if it is, then you get the chance to reap the rewards for just the cost of a stamp!

STORES AND THEIR PRICING METHODS

I remember the days before coupons. The dark days when I would blindly walk through the store and toss our key "staples" into my cart without so much as looking at what the price might be.

Why would I do this? Because these were the things that we used each and every week and I bought them because I *always* bought them!

Sound familiar? Yeah…I thought it might.

Well, here is the problem with this approach. Believe it or not, grocery prices fluctuate, even when items aren't on sale. In fact, in the standard grocery store the majority of the items will have a price change from week to week be it up or down. How much? Well, depending on the product, you could be looking at anywhere from a few pennies to a dollar or more.

To give you an idea of what I'm talking about here, let me tell you a bit about my friend Ann and one of the "must-have" items on her weekly list…none other than the family favorite and kid friendly staple of Matahama Rice.

Ann's kids love rice and through trial and error she found that the small bags of Matahama Rice were the hands down favorite in her house. So much so that she always found at least a bag or two working their way on to her weekly grocery list. The rice isn't expensive, around a $1.00 a bag, so she didn't pay any attention to those little printed numbers on the shelf as she tossed her weekly ration into the cart.

Then, one day, Ann discovered couponing. For her, the entire process was like being reunited with a long, lost friend and she has never looked back. As part of this journey she started keeping track of a few specific prices each week, her rice being one of those items.

Here's what she learned. Over a 12-week period the price of her favorite rice ranged from $0.99 per bag all the way up to $1.29 per bag. Percentage wise this is a pretty substantial difference....roughly 30%!

Now, in this case we are talking about 30% on an item that costs about $1.00, but imagine rolling this number out through the rest of your grocery list.

My friends, this is where smart shopping comes into play. Even if you never use the first coupon, this is a smart habit for any price conscious shopper. Taking the time to track the prices of your favorite items will give you the knowledge to recognize a rock bottom price when you see one and use that opportunity to stock your shelves.

So is there any rhyme or reason to these price changes? Absolutely! Some items, like rice, will trend up and down based on the current crop or on the world market as a whole. But who really has the time to keep track of that? **A simpler method is to keep the 3-month rule in mind.** Generally the grocery industry operates on a sort of quarterly cycle. If you were to keep track of a specific item during that time frame you should be able to get a clear idea of both the high and the low price.

Then, once you have those numbers in mind you know exactly what to watch for in terms of a good deal. You may not be into stockpiling, and that's fine, but you can take advantage of the low price to buy a little extra and save yourself some money in the long run.

ORGANIZING YOUR COUPONING LIFE

Later in the book you will find a whole chapter filled to the brim with brilliant organizational gems, and I highly encourage you to read it. But this issue is just too important to gloss over at this point. The reality is that couponing takes time. And, it can take *a lot* of time if you don't have some kind of system in place to both use and organize your coupons.

The choices are many, but I urge you to take the time to find what works for you and then stick with it. Not doing so will quickly leave you overwhelmed and frustrated with the process as a whole. So check out our tips and use them to build the couponing system of your dreams.

COUPON ABBREVIATIONS

Have you ever heard of the coupon language? I liken it almost to texting! Let me give you an example: I'm going to Wags, using my RR's and Q's and then running to RA to redeem my +Ups. One word: confusing! If there were any page to bookmark in this book, it's this one. This page will act almost like a decoder. If I reference something that you don't understand, check this page first! Here is a list of abbreviations and short hand that will help you decode the world of couponing:

$.75/1	–	$.75 off 1 product
$.50/2	–	$.50 off 2 products
AR	–	After Rebate
B1G1 or BOGO	–	Buy One Get One Free
B5G1	–	Buy FIVE Get One Free
BC/AC	–	Before/After Coupons
Blinkie	–	SmartSource machine with a red blinking light on it. Coupons are thus referred to as 'Blinkies'
BTFE	–	Box Tops for Education
CAT	–	Coupon that prints from a Catalina machine at the register.
CC	–	Concealed Cash
CH	–	Clearing House
CLFE	–	Campbell's Labels For Education
C/O	–	Cents Off
CRT	–	Cash register tape (receipt)
DB	–	The WeUseCoupons.com Coupon Database
DEAD	–	Refers to a dead deal, or that the offer is no longer valid
DND	–	Do Not Double
ECB	–	Extra Care Buck (earned at CVS)
ENVIE	–	Envelope
ES	–	Easy Saver, seen at Walgreens rebate booklet
ETS	–	Excludes Trial Sizes
EX or X	–	Expires on
FAR	–	Free after rebate
FC	–	First class postage stamps
FS	–	Free Shipping
FSOT	–	For Sale or Trade

GC	–	*Gift Card*
GDA	–	*Good Deal Alert*
GM	–	*General Mills Insert, a booklet of coupons that appears in newspapers every month or two.*
HBA	–	*Health & Beauty Section in the store*
INSERTS	–	*Coupon booklets found in the Sunday paper*
IP	–	*Internet Printable coupon*
ISO	–	*In Search Of (basically you need it)*
IVC	–	*Instant value coupons – seen in Walgreens rebate booklet*
MFR	–	*Manufacturer*
MIR	–	*Mail In Rebate*
MQ	–	*Manufacturer coupon*
MRP	–	*Manufacturer's retail price*
NED	–	*No Expiration Date*
OAS	–	*A Coupon that is good on one Purchase, Any Size*
OOP	–	*Out Of Pocket*
OYNO	–	*On Your Next Order*
P&G	–	*Proctor & Gamble (Sunday Booklet Coupons)*
Peelie	–	*Coupon found attached to a product. You have to peel it off.*
POP	–	*Proof of purchase*
PSA	–	*Prices Starting At*
Q	–	*Coupon*
QQ	–	*Coupon Queen*
RA	–	*Rite Aid*
RC	–	*Rain-check*
RP	–	*Red Plum (Sunday Booklet Coupons) (formerly Valassis)*

RR   –   *Register Reward from Walgreens – use as a $ off coupon on your next purchase*

SCR   –   *Rite Aid Single Check Rebate*

SRP   –   *Suggested retail price*

SS   –   *Smart Source (Sunday Booklet Coupons)*

STACKING   –   *Often stores will allow the use of more than one coupon per item, IF the coupon itself does not restrict such usage. (Usually store Q + mfr Q)*

SUPER DOUBLES or DOUBLES   –   *Coupons that are doubled $1 + in value (IE, a $1 coupon – $2, etc)*

TEARPAD   –   *A pad of forms/coupons found hanging from a store shelf or display*

TMF   –   *Try Me Free – mail in rebate for full amount of product*

TRIPLE COUPON   –   *A coupon that a grocery store triples in value*

UPC   –   *Universal Product Code, barcode on the product*

WAGS   –   *Walgreens*

WM   –   *Wal-Mart*

WUC   –   *We Use Coupons (refers to the coupon website)*

WYB   –   *When You Buy*

HOW TO USE COUPONS

Once you have your coupons and have them organized then it is time for the fun part: using them!

But how? How can you take these little slips of paper and turn them into huge grocery savings? Well, let me give you six basics rules on using coupons.

1. You can only use ONE manufacturer's coupon per item. This is almost always true. Often the coupon will specify that it is a $1.00 off 2 items. You must buy two items and can only use 1 coupon for those 2 items.

2. Depending on the store, you may be able to combine one manufacturer's coupon with a store coupon for the same item. This is the rare instance where you can use two coupons on one item.

3. Beware and read your coupon. Many coupons will say 'any' product. Look for the smallest product because the margin of savings will be better. Many coupons are specific about quantity or weight. Make sure to use coupons correctly.

4. Watch your store limits. Many stores will let you use as many coupons as you would like, while other stores limit the number of identical coupons you can use in a single transaction. Check with your stores!

5. Never give a cashier a coupon that you know will scan when the matching item was not purchased. That is called **coupon fraud**! This hurts the cashier, other coupon users, and you.

6. Watch and know which stores double and which do not. Sometimes stores will double the first two of an identical coupon and honor the rest at face value. Know your store!

These are the six basic rules of intro couponing. I often liken couponing to chess: knowing how the pieces move won't make you a good chess player. The same is true with couponing.

COUPON WORDING

Let's take a minute to talk about coupon wording. As you may have noticed, couponers have a language all their own, one that, while it makes sense to them, might as well be ancient Greek to the general public. But if you want to get the most out of your coupons, then you need to know what to look for and what all those random letters and numbers mean.

First off, as mentioned previously, before you head out to the store, you need to do some research as to the coupon polices of your specific store. These will vary from chain to chain and sometimes even from store to store depending on how much discretion is given to the individual store manager. Having this policy in hand will let you know how many coupons you can use in a single transaction, how many coupons the store is willing to double or if they double at all, if the store accepts competitor coupons and if they will allow you to stack a store coupon with a manufacturer's coupon. Now, I want to jump in and say that if some of these terms seem a bit confusing now, don't get too worried about it. We are going to cover each of these topics in detail before the end of the chapter.

For now, we want to focus on wording. Let's talk about what the coupon actually says, and what that means to you.

Things to look for:

- **VALUE**

What is your coupon worth? This will be spelled out for you in big letters front and center on every coupon, and it's important that you take the time to read each one. For example, your coupon might be for $.50 off any one Pillsbury Cinnamon roll. This means that you can use one coupon for each can of Pillsbury Cinnamon rolls that you buy.

However, if the coupon stated that it was for $.50 off any two Pillsbury Cinnamon rolls, then you would have to buy two separate cans to redeem your savings.

Why does this matter? For two reasons: First, you want to know exactly what your savings are going to be. If you are planning on $.50 off of one and it ends up being $.50 off of two, that's a pretty significant difference. Second, if you don't buy the right quantity, then the store will not allow you to use your coupon.

- **PRODUCT**

The next thing to look at is what is the coupon **for**. By this I mean is it for any Pillsbury Cinnamon rolls, or is it for Pillsbury Grand's Cinnamon rolls? This makes a difference. Make sure to just pay attention and make sure that the items in your cart and the items on your coupons match up. First, because it is the ethical thing to do, and second, because it's the only way that they will work.

- **EXPIRATION DATE**

All good things must come to an end and that is the case with even our very favorite coupons. 99.9% of all coupons you come across will have some kind of expiration date. Yes, there may be the odd exception floating around out there to prove me wrong, but I can promise it's not something you will see with any kind of regularity.

Watch the dates to make sure that your coupons are in date before you try to use them. Trying to use an expired coupon will only lead to a higher grocery bill when your cashier rejects it during checkout. Also, if you come across a rare coupon for an item that your family loves, then keep an extra close eye on that expiration date. You don't want it to expire on you before you get a chance to take advantage of the savings.

SAVINGS TIP:

If a coupon expires on June 3rd, you can use it on June 3rd until midnight.

- **SPECIAL TERMS**

As you look over your coupon you may come across a box that states "Do Not Double." This is something to make note of. Why? Because your store may have a policy against doubling or tripling coupons with this type of wording, while other stores may double it regardless. Either way it is something to pay attention to so you can accurately budget your shopping trip.

DOUBLING A COUPON

The first step to using coupons is to understand how they work in different situations and at different stores.

Let's take a look at a grocery store for example. The thing about grocery stores is that many of them double manufacturers coupons up to a certain amount. $.50, $.60 even $.99 cents, the amount can vary, but the result is the same in that you receive a higher level of savings on your purchase.

The key is to educate yourself on the policies of the specific store you plan to shop at. Some stores only double a certain number of coupons, some double on certain days and some have confusing systems that you would be better off marking on a calendar than trying to memorize. Still others have a limit of identical or like coupons per purchase. Truly the policies vary from chain to chain and at times even from store to store. But at the end of the day, it doesn't matter what their system is, you just have to know it.

This is why it is so important that you take the time to familiarize yourself with the store policies before you make the trip. Doing so will save you a large amount of time and hassle at the checkout and will be greatly appreciated by both your cashier and the store itself.

SAVINGS TIP:

If you are unsure of a store's coupon policy, ASK. Generally a store will have a copy of the policy.

Also, don't assume that policies are set in stone. Make a habit of checking and rechecking the policies as they are prone to changing without notice. And, I always make a point of carrying a printed copy of the store's policies with me when

I shop. Then I know exactly what I am dealing with and what parameters I have to keep in mind as I fill my cart.

STORE COUPONS

Where a manufacturers coupon is printed for use on a specific product, store coupons take things one-step further. They are printed for a specific product at a specific store. These types of coupons generally cannot be doubled and, other than in rare cases, they can only be used at the store in question.

Now, some stores do accept competitor coupons. These policies vary from store to store and are often extremely specific so pay attention. Doing so can save you large amounts of money. Not doing so can lead to a fantastic headache.

So how can you tell the difference between a store coupon and a manufacturers coupon? Simple! Most store coupons will say, 'Store Coupons'. Often times they will have a store logo on the coupon itself, but make sure to double check. Sometimes coupons have a logo but say Manufacturer's coupon. Chances are if you get it from the store, it's *probably* a store coupon.

STACKING

Stacking is a process of using a store coupon and a manufactures coupon on the same item. Can you do this? Yes. Is it allowed? Yes….at certain stores. Remember the whole thing about checking policies? That is very important here.

Here's how it works. Many stores, especially grocery stores, will allow you to use one store and one manufactures coupon per item. This is a great thing! It allows you to double your savings as long as you shop smart!

Now, remember when we were talking about store coupons and how some stores would accept competitor coupons? This is where you can use those policies to your couponing advantage. For example, many Publix stores will accept one like competitor coupon per item. What constitutes a competitor? Well, that is something that you have to check on a store-by-store basis, but it almost always includes Target. This means that if Target has a printable coupon that corresponds with a current Publix promotion, then you can take advantage of those savings and achieve the rock bottom prices you are looking for.

COUPON SHORTHAND

When you go online to check out coupon websites you might notice that we have our very own shorthand for explaining what is on sale in a current week and where you might find the coupons you want. Now, I want to take just a minute to decode the lingo and let you know what you are looking at.

For example, if Dawn Dishwashing Liquid were on sale at Publix 10 for $10, then you might see a note that looked something like this:

- Dawn Dishwashing Liquid 10/$10 –
- $.50/1 Dawn Dishwashing Liquid, PG 9/02

Make sense? Well, let's break it down. The first part is simple. It is telling you that Dawn is on sale for $1.00 each. That is what 10 for $10 means. At most stores it doesn't mean that you have to buy 10 of an item to get the price, it just means that they have it on sale for $1 each.

Next, there is a coupon for $.50 off of 1 Dawn and you can find it in the Proctor and Gamble insert from September 2nd.

Let's look at another:

- Colgate Toothpaste BOGO - $1.00
- $.50/1 Colgate Toothpaste, SS 10/13

This means that Colgate Toothpaste is on sale buy one get one free. The sale price is $1.00. You can find a $.50 off of one coupon for Colgate toothpaste in the October 13th SmartSource insert.

The main things to look at here are the value, what the coupon is for, where it came from (i.e. what insert) and when it came out. This tells you everything you need to know to find this coupon and helps you to figure what your final price will be on the item in question.

In this type of short hand Proctor and Gamble is always written as PG, SmartSource is SS and Red Plum is RP. You may occasionally see different inserts pop up from time to time, but these are the big three.

BOGO SALES

Buy one get one free deals are some of the best deals out there! Did you know that you can sweeten the deal by using coupons on those sales? First, let's talk about the two types of BOGO sale that you may see in the store:

- Traditional BOGO Sales:
- Percentage off BOGO Sales

At most stores, if you see a sale or advertisement for a buy one get one free sale, you purchase one and the other is free. That is a traditional BOGO sale. Now to sweeten the deal you can do a few things. First, some stores allow you to use a BOGO free coupon on top of the sale, which results in both products being free. The store gets reimbursed for the manufacturer coupon and the transaction is still profitable for the store! Remember to check each store's coupon policy, but most stores allow this. The next option is to ask if you can use a coupon on each item being purchased. Some stores allow you to only use one coupon on a BOGO sale, while others allow two coupons (even though the second item is free) because you are buying two items. If you can use two coupons, you will end up spending very little for both items!

Certain stores have BOGO sales, but you don't have to buy 2 to get the sale price. You purchase one, and it rings up half price. This is odd to think about, because in reality they should not be called BOGO but 50% off sales. This generally will occur in the Southern US at stores like Publix, Bi-Lo, and Harris Teeter to name a few. With sales like this, you are almost always allowed to use two coupons, which drives the cost of the items down dramatically.

These types of sales are crucial to the type of huge coupon savings that you see from the extreme couponers. In truth, the sale is the bulk of the savings because it represents the rock bottom price for the product in question. When you find that rock bottom price and are able to pair it with a high value coupon, then you will be able to achieve the huge savings that you are looking for.

Truthfully, it's a bit like a puzzle!

SPECIAL PROMOTIONS/SALES

Occasionally various stores will run special promotions or sales that are the stuff of couponing dreams. Here are a few good examples that I have come across.

- Kmart doubling 5 coupons up to $2.00 per transaction
- Bi-Lo honoring an ad misprint that announced double coupons up to $0.99
- Various stores offering a set amount of money off your total purchase. i.e. $10.00 off a pre coupon $50.00 purchase.

It is critical to take advantage of these sales with your coupons! Coupons can usually be combined with these special promotions because they (the promotions) are coming from different places. One is a store promotion, the other (a coupon) is from the manufacturer! This will result in tremendous savings!

THE "ANY" COUPON

Have you ever seen a coupon for $1.00 off **any** xxx product? These are great coupons because they don't have size limitations! Why is that important, well it's simple. The smaller products you buy, more you affect the unit cost with a coupon. Let me give you an example. Say I need deodorant. I have 4 coupons. The value size deodorant is priced at $3.49 and it contains 2 regular sized deodorants. The regular size (2.0oz packaged individually) is priced at $1.99. Then we have the small size which is only 1oz and is priced at $1.19. Remember you can use a coupon on each item, but only one coupon. Let me show you a scenario if I have a coupon for $1 off ANY deodorant:

Value Size Package 4oz	Regular Package 2oz	Small Package 1oz
Price: $3.49	Price: $1.99	Price: $1.19
Coupon: -$1	Coupon: -$1 (two coupons allowed)	Coupon: -$1 four coupons allowed
Unit Cost: $2.49	Unit Cost: $.99	Unit Cost: $.19
Final Cost for 4oz: $2.49	Final Cost for 4oz: $1.98	Final Cost for 4oz: $.76

As you can see, the power of buying smaller and using the ANY coupon is very effective. I personally would much rather spend $.76 for the four ounces of deodorant than $2.49. Remember when you find any coupon, look and see if it's worth buying smaller.

WRAP UP

Is your brain spinning yet? Don't worry, it will all start making sense, especially after you make that first trip to the store and see your new system in action.

It is a lot to take in and I understand that. Trust me, I know plenty of people who head off to the store, coupons in hand, only to turn right around and leave again when they get overwhelmed or intimidated by the whole process.

But you have a secret weapon. You've got this book and we are just getting started.

Next we are going to look at how to get started, stockpiling, how to organize your coupons and how you can take it to the extreme. Basically I am going to show you how you can make couponing work for you. How it can fit into your schedule, into your life and into your budget. It's possible, I know it is; now we just have to make it happen.

Chapter Four
A Method to the Madness

I've given numerous interviews to newspapers and TV programs and do you know my number one tip for beginning couponers? It's organization. By far, a savings system is critical to your savings success. Get a system. In this chapter, we will cover how to clip your coupons, discover organizational systems that are popular with couponers, and how to find a system that works for you.

Sounds simple doesn't it? And, it is. But the first time you stare down at a stack of 10 inserts deep, it can be more than a little intimidating! So we are going to put a method to the madness and help you make the most out of every single couponing minute!

HOW TO CLIP YOUR COUPONS

Seem like a no brainer? Well, there is a little more to this than you might think, especially for those of you who want to make things as easy as possible. If this sounds like you, then check out the steps below for making the most of your coupon clipping time!

1. Separate your inserts.

Buying multiple copies of the Sunday paper doesn't mean that you have to sign on for cutting out the same insert over and over and over again. Not in the least. Remember, the idea here is to work smarter rather than harder!

So instead we are going to separate our inserts out so that we only have to do the work once and still get to enjoy the full benefit of each and every coupon in our stash.

Here is what I mean when I say to separate the inserts:

- Find a large open surface like your dining room table or living room floor.
- Open all of your papers and remove the inserts. Separate them into piles in front of you. If you had 5 papers and each was stuffed with 1 Red Plum and 1 SmartSource, you should now have 2 piles of 5 inserts each. One for Red Plum and one for SmartSource pile.
- Pick an insert, say SmartSource.
- Take the top insert and separate it out so that each page is starting its own pile.
- Repeat this process with the remaining 4 SmartSource inserts until you have individual piles for each page.
- Neatly stack your pages.

2. Staple the coupons.

Once your inserts are separated, then it is time to staple the coupons. To do this pick up each pile individually and staple through the picture on *each* coupon. This will help keep like coupons together after they are cut and keep you from having to constantly search for individuals that manage to escape.

Note that it is important to staple through the picture. Why? Because in terms of redeeming the coupons, the picture doesn't really matter. What does matter are the words. If you staple through the small print, the expiration date or even the wording that denotes the value of the coupon then know that these areas may tear and make it where your cashier cannot read the coupon. If they can't read the coupon, then there is a good chance that they won't accept it.

3. Cut the coupons

Once all your coupons are stapled, now it is time to cut. With this method you only have to cut each insert one time since you have stacked and stapled all like pages together. Just don't get sloppy! If you cut off a bar code or expiration date then, again, there is a good chance that the store will not accept the coupon. So take care! Remember, these little beauties are like cash and you don't want to do anything that would make them lose their value.

4. Sort the coupons.

Now that everything is stacked, stapled and clipped it's time to store. How? Well that is up to you, but I'll give you a few good tips right in the next section.

HOW TO ORGANIZE YOUR COUPONS

I'm going to let you in on a little secret. Coupons? They can make a **huge mess**. One that you don't even want to think about let alone face. Here's the danger. You can spend all the time in the world putting together your shopping trip, but if you don't have some kind of organizational system in place, you might as well throw your coupons up in the air and watch them rain down like confetti!

How can you avoid this bleak future? Well, there are several different options that hardcore couponers rely on, and I am going to cover 3. These are **not** the only options out there, but I find that they are the most common and so probably the most effective. I will say this: each method has its pros and cons, so I'll be sure to cover both. Then it's up to you to choose the system that works best for you!

Binder

The binder system is just what it sounds like. You start with a nice thick binder, a couple sets of dividers and a few packs of baseball card holders. From there you pick your categories and sort your coupons.

Each stapled pile of coupons is slipped down into a baseball card slot and you get to flip through and see exactly what you have on hand.

Pros:

- Easy to Organize. Everything is right in front of you.
- Easy to Use. Again, if you can see what you have then it is easy to keep track of what coupons you have on hand.

- Portable. Binders are a great way to take every coupon you have with you each and every time you walk out the door.

Cons:

- Heavy. These babies can get some weight on them when they are full!
- Bulky. It can be difficult to situate your binder in the shopping cart where it is secure yet you can also easily turn the pages.
- Not Secure. If you accidentally pick your binder up the wrong way, you may just get to watch all your coupons flutter to the floor!

The binder system is what I recommend for beginning couponers. It works, it's what I used and until you develop a system of your own, that fits your unique needs, the binder is a fantastic way to get and stay organized.

Tips for binder users, sort your binder by aisle in the store. Imagine simply walking down each aisle and flipping the pages in your coupon binder. The savings are right at your finger tips. Binders can easily be sorted by category and it's up to you which categories you'd like it to contain.

Accordion File

Remember these? I think that just about everyone's mom had one stuffed in her purse at one time or another, a little checkbook sized file that fit into her purse to be pulled out at the strangest moments.

These days the accordion file has undergone a face-lift. Now they come in all shapes, sized and colors and they can be pretty useful in terms of organizing your coupon stash.

Let's look at the pros and cons!

Pros:

- Portable. These small files fit into your purse and are easy to carry anywhere.
- Lightweight. May not seem like a big deal….until you try hauling around one of those mondo coupon binders!
- Versatile. It is easy and affordable to change things up in your accordion file. Binder? Not so much!

Cons:

- Disorganized. Even the most dedicated organizer will have trouble finding what she is looking for with this system.
- Cluttered. With the large number of coupons that most serious couponers have on hand, these little files fill up fast!
- Easy to Lose. Are you prone to laying down your keys and walking off? How about your cell phone? I promise, this won't be any better. It's just this time you'll have hours of work in it and you'll leave on a grocery store shelf rather than a restaurant table.

Clip-less Method

Before I go further, I'd like to say that the clip-less method is a method that more established couponers use. If you are interested in this method, try it, but know that I recommend the coupon binder for beginners

The clip-less method is used by couponers that don't have time to clip, or feel that clipping is overwhelming. They find a filing cabinet and sort their coupon inserts by date and type. Example: June 10th, P&G would be in one folder, while the June 10th Redplum would be in another. When they find an item they want or need, they simply go back, clip what they need. Couponers that use this system rely heavily on our coupon database to aid them in their search for coupons.

Pros:
- Less time. No clipping all the coupons, just clip when you need them
- Easy. No issues with losing coupons or organizing

Cons:
- You are not able to shop with your coupons at the store. This requires research before ever stepping foot in the store
- Inability to stock up on clearance items. If you find a surprise sale, you are out of luck because your coupons are at home. You must make a return trip.

MY STEPS FOR ORGANIZING YOUR SHOPPING TRIP

We are going to look at how to organize just your regular run of the mill weekly shopping trip. I'll tell you right now that there are several ways to go about this and there is no way I can cover them all.

1. Check Out the Weekly Ads

The first step to planning any trip is to check out what's for sale in a given week. Once you know what's for sale then you can sort through and find the items that interest you. What makes this new way to couponing different than grandma's is that we have one powerful tool that she didn't: the internet. Part of my weekly ritual is to check coupon blogs and see what is on sale. They will often times provide lists that will be pre-matched with coupons to make your life easier. Get online, and save time!

2. Make Your List

This part is pretty straightforward. As you look through the ads, decide which items you want and what stores you want to visit. From there you make your list. Make sure you note which coupons you want to use on each item as well as the price. You want to know what the shelf price should be as well as the final price after all coupons have been used.

Also, make a note of any items that you will be stacking coupons on. If this is the plan, then you need to have both the store and the manufacturer coupons in hand before heading out the door.

3. Pull Your Coupons

It's time to pull your coupons. Now, I know many people that just prefer to shop with their full binders and pull as they go, but this is more of a time commitment than I want to make. Yes, I generally have my binder with me, but if I go ahead and pull the coupons I **know** I want to use before hand, then I can save myself a ton of time in the store.

Saving time is always a win in my book!

At this point I usually fold my list in half and stick the coupons inside to make sure everything stays together. I have also used an envelope to keep different stores separated out.

I know other people who use small accordion folders for this task. It really doesn't matter which system you use so long as you find the one that works for you and you stick with it.

4. Bring Your Binder

Even though I don't shop from my binder I always make sure to have it on hand. Why? Because every single time I leave it at home I always find some unadvertised deal that makes me wish I had it! So lug it in with you. It may end up hanging out at the bottom of the cart for the day, but it's better to have it and not need it than need it and not have it!

You may be asking, why don't you shop from your binder? Becoming successful with couponing, and truly saving on your grocery bill means that I have laser like precision in the grocery store. I go in with a list. I know how much things should cost. I have my coupons already ready. I collect my items, pay and walk out. That works for me, but others prefer to shop from their binder, not pulling coupons until they see the price of the product. Do what works for *you*!

5. Finishing Up

If there is one thing I want to make sure you realize about organization it's that you have to find a system that works for you. (Am I starting to sound like a broken record?)

And here's why. Trying to force yourself into a system that makes sense to someone else is like shoving a round peg into a square hole. It doesn't work and it's a good way to make you more than slightly crazy. I don't know about you, but I can promise that I have more than enough to worry about throughout my day without trying to make sense of an organizational system that doesn't match up with my needs.

So I don't try.

It may take some experimenting, I know it did for me, but you will find the choice that works for you. And, once you do, stick with it. Because the last thing you want is a month's worth of coupons hanging out at the bottom of a bag where you stuffed them and then forgot about them. Unless you just like clipping coupons for the fun of it. In that case, go nuts!

Chapter Five
Taking it to the Extreme

Show of hands, how many of you have heard of a TV show called *Extreme Couponing*?

Yep, thought that might be the case. But, for those of you who aren't familiar, *Extreme Couponing* is a TLC show that documents the shopping trips of different couponers who tend to go above and beyond. They don't just coupon, they have it down to a science and they are regularly able to snag the items that their families want and need for a fraction of what it would normally cost.

I guess that it's time to mention that I have been featured on *Extreme Couponing*....twice.

But this process isn't just about getting a good deal. For me, and for my family, couponing is a way of life. More so, for us, it has been life changing. As you know, these little slips of paper have changed the way I look at money and have completely revitalized my finances. So what other people may call "extreme" I call "planning." I call it taking advantage of the knowledge that I have and being prepared for what may come next.

Now, I also know that some of you will not be interested in this part of couponing in the least, and that's fine. But for others, this is what you've been waiting for. Now we are going to talk about taking your savings to the next level. It's not rocket science, but it does take planning and more than a little attention to detail.

One thing I would like to mention about the TV show is to remember that it's a television show. I can't promise you 90% off your grocery bill. Some aspects of the show are not realistic. After all who really needs 40 bottles of mustard that they may not consume, unless they are donating it and it was **free**. My version of extreme couponing is designed to help you lower your grocery bill dramatically, buy things your family actually needs and hopefully have you spending 50% less than you were on groceries. But don't expect to be able to duplicate the savings from TV.

WHAT DOES *EXTREME* MEAN?

The first thing to look at is what does it mean to be an *extreme* couponer? Does it mean that you only go for the items that are free? Does it mean that you buy huge quantities of any and every sale that you come across? Does it mean that you have enough toilet paper stashed beneath your son's bed to wrap the earth?

It could mean all of these things, or none of them. See, extreme couponing is as individualized as general couponing, it's just on a bigger scale. It means that you are bumping up your efforts and really looking at the big overall picture rather than just your weekly trip to the store. In fact, many of the strategies we have or will discuss in this book may be viewed as extreme by one individual or another.

And that's fine.

After all, my goal is not to turn you all into little couponing robot copies of myself. My goal is to give you knowledge to become the type of couponer that you want to be. If others call that extreme, I'm okay with that. Let them pay full price.

SO WHAT DOES IT MEAN TO BE AN EXTREME COUPONER?

I'll give you my own personal definition. For me it comes down to quantity and storage. Those of us who know how much toothpaste, toilet paper and oatmeal that our families use in six months to a year and make a point to keep that amount on hand probably fall into the extreme category.

Not that it's a bad thing, it just means that you are probably shopping on a larger scale than the person next to you.

HOW TO GO FOR IT

Now that we know what it means to be extreme, let's look at how to get the job done. After all, this type of trip takes planning and preparation if you don't want to end up with sticker shock after all the dust settles.

It's a process, and one that you will have to refine to meet your needs, but I'll share the basic steps I take before each trip out the door.

There are two main parts to extreme couponing: the sales and the coupons. Either could be argued as the most important, but to me, one really doesn't matter all that much without the other. After all, it is the combination of two that we are looking for. That magic mixture where we can snag optimal savings on all our favorite goodies.

FIND THE SALES

First, let's talk about the sales. Extreme couponing is, at its heart, the ability to match up sales with coupons and special store incentives, and then obtain a sizeable amount of product, which they will consume, for very little money.

So, the first step in this process is to know what sales are out there. There are several ways to do this. You can get your hands on the store fliers, search online or go to the store and check. All viable though with different amounts of time involved.

Personally I go for the online method. It's not foolproof, but it's a great place to start and they often have the ads out for you to see a full day before you could pick them up at the store.

Now, when I say find the sales, I mean just that. If you are going to take this to the extreme, then you have to open yourself up to the possibility of shopping more than one store in a week. I do recommend that you set a limit – after all, you can make yourself crazy trying to hit every deal at every store – but it is feasible to hit multiple different stores in a single week.

Why would you want to go to more than one store? Different sales. If you find 5 to 10 great items at Kroger and then another 5 to 10 at Wal-Mart then you can pick and choose as to which items would work best for your needs.

Yes, drug stores have to figure into this count as well, but that is a whole different animal and not one that we are going to tackle at this point.

So find the sales. Make a list of the items you are interested in and then its time to start planning your strategy.

FIND THE COUPONS

Once you have a clear idea of which items you are going after, then it is time to see what coupons you have in hand to match up. Again, many online sites will tell you exactly what coupons are out there and for me that is the easiest way to go. After all, they even have links to the printable coupons right there for you to click on. This saves you from the endless chore of hunting through your binder for each item on your list, hoping that you have something to match up. Also, make sure to employ our coupon database. This is a simple and free tool to use that will locate virtually any coupon that is available.

Let's talk quantity for a moment. If you are thinking in terms of the extreme couponer, then you are probably going to want more than one or two of a given item. Which means that you will need more than one or two coupons to work with.

The question is, how many do you need?

It's a question only you can answer, but one that you need to think about before you head out the door to buy your Sunday papers. After all, it is a cost, one that must be counted in order to have a full picture of your grocery budget.

Do I think that you need 100 papers every Sunday? No. Not only would that be a nightmare to sort through, but as we've seen, most stores have a strict limit as to how many like coupons you can use in a single transaction. With that in mind I'm going to recommend 4-8 to start with. It's a nice round number that fits with many store polices and in most cases it will give you enough items to work with from week to week.

If you find that 4-8 is not enough, then you can always go up later, but I don't want you to jump in with both feet and land over your head.

At this point we know what the sales are and we have our coupons matched up and in hand. We are closer to walking out the door, but still not quite there to make this an extreme shopping trip. There is still work to do.

KNOW THE POLICIES

The next thing to consider is your store's policies. What are their coupon policies? Is there a limit per transaction? How do they feel about multiple transactions? Do they offer different sales and incentives on different days? When do they re-stock? When do the new sales go live? Truly the list goes on and on.

It sounds like a lot to think about, and it is, but I promise that it will become second nature before long.

But, I don't just want to throw this list at you, I want to tell you why it matters. Why should you care about the answers to all these questions? Because the answers make the difference between couponing and extreme couponing.

As an extreme couponer, you have to take every detail into account before you shop. Knowing when your store restocks their shelves will give you a better chance at getting the items you are after. Some stores will only allow you to take advantage of a certain deal once per day, meaning that you will either have to take extra people with you or plan on multiple trips. And, if your store only doubles coupons one day a week, then you need to know that. You'll also need to get there early before the shelves are stripped of every good deal in sight.

Knowing your store's policies is more than just knowing how they feel about coupons. It's knowing how the store works. Then it's knowing how you can make it work for you.

Now we are one step closer to actually walking out the door. You know what you want. You know what coupons you have and you know the best time to go based on the store you shop at. You also know who you need to take with you. Now it's time to make a plan.

Wait? Haven't we already been doing that?

Not even close!

MAKE A PLAN

When shopping like an extreme couponer, you need to have a detailed plan in place for each shopping trip. This is much more than just an average shopping list; it is a strategy that covers you from the moment you walk into the store all the way through to loading your car.

Your plan should include:

- Price for each item on your list both before and after coupons.
- Quantity you want for each item as well as the coupons you have to use.

- Notes about any moneymakers and the effect they should have on your overall out of pocket cost.
- List of multiple transactions and what each transaction should include.
- Any special sales or incentives for the day/week

Basically you need a plan of attack. You need to know what you are going for and how much it should cost you when it's all said and done. Not understanding this is a great way to leave savings on the table.

Another simple reason you need a plan: so you don't overspend! By knowing how much of an item I'm going to buy and how much it should cost, I get a rough idea of how much I'm going to spend! That is a great asset when you are trying to control your grocery budget.

EXECUTE

Now, after all that, you are ready to go. It's finally time to walk out the door and head to the store to put these new practices in action. But your work isn't done. It's time for vigilance. Even though you have checked every price and matched every coupon, you still have to ensure that the price on the shelf matches the price in your notes.

Find an item out of stock? Make a note to ask for a rain check. Item not ringing up for the right price? Point it out. It is these small details which are often over looked yet they are the one that add up to the huge savings you are looking for.

As an extreme couponer you have to pay attention during check out to make sure that each item is scanning correctly, that all your coupons are in order and accepted and that your final total is in line with your very detailed plan. The magic happens at the checkout, but you must watch the magic!! Don't let a cashier mistakenly miss a coupon. It's your job to pay attention, not theirs.

And then, you get ready to do it all again at the very next stop.

PRACTICALITIES

When you talk about extreme couponing, you're talking about the trip to the store, about the fun of watching that total drop and drop until practically nothing is left and you can pay for your groceries with the change in your pocket. I'm kidding here, but you get the picture.

What people don't often think about is the practicality of buying, transporting and storing that amount of product.

It's an issue! One I can promise you want to think about before you're standing in front of your small two-door car with two huge carts full of groceries that you've somehow managed to steer all the way through the parking lot without banging into half a dozen cars on the way out.

So now let's take a moment to talk about the practicalities of extreme couponing and how you might want to come up with a plan before you ever head out to the store.

TRANSPORTATION

Once you buy all your goodies, you then have to get them home. So, if you have a small car, or even a large car that is often cluttered with the reality of life, then you may want to make sure that it's cleaned out. Basically you have to make sure that everything you buy will fit and you can get it all home in a single trip.

It sounds silly I know, but more than once I have seen someone standing in a parking lot with a very bewildered look on their face as they looked back and forth between their overflowing carts and their very tiny car.

STORAGE

The last thing to think about is storage. After all you don't want your groceries to spoil once you go through all the time and effort attributed to this type of extreme shopping trip. So if you want to buy 3-dozen yogurt cups, then make sure you have the fridge space for 3-dozen yogurt cups. Because I can promise you that your kids won't be excited about a dinner plate decorated with nothing more than the three flavors of yogurt that you can't stuff into the fridge.

You should also have storage in mind for the non-perishables. Maybe it's a set of shelves in the garage. Or it could be a large pantry. You could even take over that guest room that you never set foot in. It really doesn't matter what you choose as long as the area is climate controlled and you can keep food purchases off the ground as much as possible.

We will talk more about stockpiling in a later chapter, but I still think that the reality of where you will store all these items is something to keep in mind before you ever make the first trip.

QUANTITIES

Remember to be practical. If you've seen couponers on TV buying hundreds of diapers and they don't have a child, they aren't extreme couponers. They are just plain weird, unless their purpose is to give it all away (or they are expecting). Buy what you can use and watch expiration dates. Do the math, find out what you consume. If you find a freebie that you don't or won't use, buy it any way and give it away. We'll talk about blessing others in a later chapter!

We have covered the basics. Extreme couponing, like all other types of couponing is a process. A process that will change over time and force you to adjust your shopping habits again and again. The best advice I can give you on that front is to be flexible and accept these changes as they come. It's not always fun, but getting angry and making a scene isn't going to solve anything and it's certainly not going to entice the stores to make things easier for us.

WE USE COUPONS, YOU SHOULD TOO!

Chapter Six

Stockpiling 101:
Why You Need to Buy 10 Toothpastes!

Stockpiling…the giant elephant that has taken up permanent residence in the couponing room! Some people think that stockpiling equals hoarding and I'm here to tell you those people are wrong. This is the big one and this is the one that makes most outsiders think they just don't have what it takes to coupon.

It is also the one that separates the men from the boys when it comes to utilizing coupons to yield drastic changes in your weekly, monthly and even yearly grocery budget.

And at this point, I've heard it all! Let's see if any of these excuses start to ring a bell:

- "Stockpiling? I can't do that! Where would I put it?"
- "That's hoarding!"

- "Why would I buy 10 tubes of toothpaste when I can just go back to the store next week and get another one?"
- "10 tubes of toothpaste? That's just crazy!"
- "That stuff will expire before I can use it!"

Yep, each of these objections have worked their way into one or a hundred conversations in the last few years! But now we are going to put them to rest as we move forward and gain understanding of both what stockpiling is, and why it is absolutely essential to an effective couponing strategy.

So, to start things off and give you a clear mental picture of why you should stockpile I'm going to introduce you to a good friend of mine. Her name is Amy and she is a parent just like many of you and me. The difference is that Amy has 4 little ones running around her house and the increasingly difficult challenge of bringing food to the table led her to embrace couponing in the last year.

At first, Amy fought against the idea of a stockpile. She didn't have room for any kind of major food storage and it was difficult for her to let go of her trusty weekly shopping list.

In short, Amy was in a rut.

The defining moment came over a box of oatmeal. See, Amy had done the math and she knew that her family of 6 went through a minimum of 2 boxes of instant oatmeal a week, sometimes a bit more, others a bit less, but an average of 2 boxes a week. With that in mind oatmeal became one of those staple items that never worked its way off her grocery list. Each week she would head to the store and pick up two boxes of oatmeal along with the other items on her list. Some weeks she was able to buy the "good" oatmeal that hers kids loved and asked for. But most of the time her family was left facing off with the hated generic brand.

There is nothing wrong with generic. Amy's kids just didn't love their oatmeal and seeing that box on the counter was always a sure fire way to elicit a strong round of heartfelt groans. Now, before we go any further, I want to take just a moment to show you the math we are talking about here:

COST BREAKDOWN:

Retail Cost of 1 Box of Oatmeal: $2.49
2 Boxes a Week x 52 Weeks A Year = 104 Boxes
104 Boxes (Year Supply) x $2.49 =

$259 ANNUAL COST FOR OATMEAL

That, my friends, is A LOT of oatmeal. In fact you may look at that number and panic a bit but keep this in mind. It may not be oatmeal, but you **all** have lurkers like this on your weekly grocery list, items that are staples in your pantry that could be purchased in advance and stockpiled for pennies. But since you have yet to embrace the idea of stockpiling, you continue to pay full or sale price for these goodies week after week after week.

Paying full price is pretty much the equivalent of pouring your hard earned money straight down the drain! It truly makes my heart hurt.

Enter couponing and stockpiling!

Amy's sister-in-law had been working for quite some time on converting her to the couponing lifestyle. Amy was hesitant, thinking it was too much work for too little reward, but she was willing to give it a try as long as her sister-in-law was willing to go with her to the store and help her through that daunting first trip.

No problem!

They left the kids with Grandma and headed out.

At the store that day Amy was introduced to a whole new way of shopping. Their "list" was built off of a combination of sale items and coupons. It was only about 5 items strong and they were looking for multiples of each and every item. For example, instead of buying 2 packs of yogurt, they picked up 10. Instead of 1 pack of fruit cups a full dozen went into the cart. And as the pile grew, so did Amy's stress level. She couldn't imagine how she was supposed to pay for all the items in the cart and she still didn't believe in the power of the coupon.

By the time they made it to the oatmeal, she had dug in her heels and balked. The oatmeal was a key item on their list that day. The sister-in-law knew that it was a big hit around Amy's house and she had 50 coupons in her binder that she was willing to share.

The price after coupons? A whopping $0.49 a box and that was for the yummy Quaker oatmeal that Amy's kids loved! But even after explaining that to Amy she was still hesitant. 50 boxes of oatmeal? Where was she supposed to put it? How was she supposed to store it? Wouldn't **that** much oatmeal go bad before her kids could manage to eat it? See even though Amy **knew** that her kids went through 2 boxes of oatmeal a week, she still couldn't wrap her mind around the idea of buying in advance. Buying for 2 weeks....maybe. But 6 full months? She couldn't do it.

COUPON SCENARIO:

25 Boxes of Oatmeal on Sale for $2.00
25 Coupons for $1.50 off 1 Box of Oatmeal
Final Cost Per Oatmeal: $.50

$12.50 FOR 25 BOXES OF OATMEAL THAT'S 80% OFF RETAIL!

In the end they compromised with 25 boxes and headed to the checkout. As the total dropped and dropped and dropped some more, Amy became more and more excited about the whole couponing thing and what she might be able to do with it. By the time the cashier looked up and said, "Your total for the entire order is $32.73," she was completely hooked. But she still was not hooked enough to go back and buy those extra 25 boxes of oatmeal.

Now let's fast-forward a bit. When Amy got home that day she was excited about her trip but still couldn't believe that she had been talked into 25 boxes of oatmeal. See, her mind was still trapped by that weekly grocery list and it was hard for her to move past it. Plus, she *knew* that when she finally ran out she would just head back to the store and pick up some more.

No big deal, right?

And she held onto that fact for the next 12 weeks. Then, one day Amy went to the cabinet to reach for a box of oatmeal and found it empty, completely empty without a single pack of oatmeal in sight. She didn't think much of it other than a passing, "Wow, that went faster than I thought it would," before walking over and adding the beloved oatmeal back onto her grocery list.

Only one problem, when Amy got back to the store that week oatmeal wasn't on sale. In fact, to get the same Quaker oatmeal that her kids had been enjoying for the last three months it was going to cost her right at $2.49 a box, the regular price!

That was the moment when Amy embraced stockpiling and finally understood what her sister-in-law had been trying to tell her for 4 straight months. When she realized that she had purchased 25 boxes of oatmeal three months earlier for almost exactly what it would cost her to buy 5 boxes today she went straight to the hardware store and picked up a set of shelves for her garage to start a stockpile.

Today, Amy has embraced the couponing lifestyle and she has never looked back! Amy understood a basic concept about stockpiling: **it's not about the stuff, it's about the price**. You see, many people hear stockpiling and immediately think hoarding. When I hear stockpiling, I think pre-buying on a low price. This idea of pre-buying items that are super cheap that you know you will need savings thousands every year.

While this is a true story, what I want you to get from it is the real difference that building a stockpile can make, and to do that we need to break things down to the cold hard cash.

So let's look at the difference here:

We already know that Amy's family goes through an average of 104 boxes of oatmeal a year. Now let's take a look at the real difference that couponing can make on just this one item.

- 104 boxes of Quaker oatmeal x $2.49 average price = $259 a year
- 104 boxes of store brand oatmeal x $2.09 average price = $217 a year
- 104 boxes of Quaker oatmeal x $.50 after coupon price = $52 a year

By making the decision to stockpile Amy can save her family over $207 per year on just this one item. Even if you are buying generic, and maybe purchase the oatmeal on sale for $2.00 a box, you would still save over $150 a year. Now just imagine what those savings would look like if they were multiplied out over the rest of her weekly grocery list!

This is what stockpiling can do for you and this is why it is the cornerstone of couponing. After all, why should you pay for something later that you can get for free or cheap today? All it costs you is a place for the item to sit until you are ready to use it.

So now we are going to talk about the steps you need to take in order to effectively build and manage your stockpile. Each one is simple, but each is also important when it comes to achieving the highest possible percentage of savings for your family.

MAKE A LIST

Before you even get started you need to sit down and take a close look at your family's buying and consuming habits. In short, you need to know what items you use on a weekly or monthly basis. Now, many of these items will come from your weekly grocery list. The items that, regardless of price you throw into the cart week after week.

These are your families "staples," the items that you use and that you make a point to keep on hand. Basically these are the items you "need" to have on hand.

The next step is to extend your list to the items you "like" to have. The ones that you enjoy and like to have on hand, but generally hold off on until you find a "good buy."

The final step is to list the items that you would "love" to have. The dream items that you only buy on special occasions but savor each and every time they come into your house.

Now, keep in mind, you won't find everything on your list on sale each and every week. That is why we stockpile after all! But, knowing what you are looking for will help you stay organized and keep you from being overwhelmed as you are getting started. Before long, you may be able to keep your list in your head, but this is always a good place to start.

KNOW YOUR LIMITS

Once you know **what** you are looking to buy, the next question is **how much**. Here's what I mean by that. When you find that rock bottom price, the one that is the lowest of the low all the way down to free, you need to know how much of that item that you want to throw into your cart. The only way to do this is to figure out how much of a particular item your family will use before that item can expire.

Back to the oatmeal example. Oatmeal generally has a shelf life of 12-18 months. Thus, all of our math for this example was based on the timeframe of 12- 18 months. If the item in question had been yogurt, then our time frame would have been vastly different. After all, you wouldn't want to buy a year's worth of yogurt just to throw it in the trash after a few short weeks, because it's expired. The idea is to save money after all! No, you would want to buy the right amount of yogurt that would last your family right up to the expiration date, thus giving you time to be on the lookout for another great sale.

I do realize that there are items out there that have no expiration date. Things like toilet paper, paper towels, dish washing detergent and laundry goodies have no real shelf life and can hang out at your house for as long as you want them around. In this case you need to decide what level of stock you are comfortable with. To do this, figure what you would use in 3, 6, 9 and 12 months and then look at the storage space you have on hand. From there decide what level you are comfortable with and try to keep yourself stocked to that level at all times. Then if you go for a long period of time without coming across a good sale you are still well stocked and not left paying full price for something that you suddenly find yourself out of.

Now, the only side note to this system is for those of you who are looking to use couponing as a way to donate to those in need. In that case you want to keep a list not only of what your family uses, but also of possible donation items. In this case your limit may not be placed according to usage. It may be based on the number of coupons you have versus the number of items that you can find.

HAVE A PLAN

Stockpiles take space. There is just no way around it. If you are going to rid yourself of the weekly grocery list and embrace a new way to shop, then you need to have a plan in place as to where you will store your bounty.

And I can promise you that taking over your kitchen counters will only work for so long!

So before you make that first trip to the store you need to have some idea of what you want to do with the items that you bring home. Some people are able to designate a room in their homes, others have to make due with a closet and still others are forced to find space whenever they can. Any of these options will work, but if you want your stockpile to be effective then you need to have it well organized so that you can keep track of what you have on hand.

One quick tip. When it comes to stockpiling, I tend to prefer shelving over bins and here's why. Bins equal piles. No matter how organized they are or how much time you put into keeping things straight, one good bump and you are left with a pile of mess. One that leaves you no real clue as to what exactly you have on hand.

Shelves allow you to organize. Not only that, but they allow you to visually keep track of the items you have on hand. Being organized and knowing what you have on hand reduces waste. And, as saving money is the end game here, reducing waste is a key to the whole puzzle.

TRACK THE CYCLE

Most shoppers have a general idea as to the average price of the items they buy each and every week. But I want you to have more than just a general idea. I want you to *know* and the only way to do this is to track prices.

Here's why.

Even without taking stores sales and coupons into consideration, prices fluctuate. And they fluctuate a lot! I have seen grocery prices fluctuate as much as 25% from one week to the next without a sale in sight. The thing is, there is a method to the madness. See, prices tend to cycle. They go up, they go down and they go on sale but they do so in a bit of a pattern. If you begin to anticipate that pattern, then you stand a better chance of always buying when an item is at its rock bottom price.

The next logical question is how do I figure out the patterns? Well, it took me a little while to figure them out, but I'll give you a leg up! Let's quickly take a look at a few items in a list and think for a moment when they should go on sale:

- Ketchup
- Cough Drops
- Soup
- Hot Dogs
- Evaporated Milk

Okay, so looking at this list, let's think about when you really use these products. Ketchup and hot dogs are the easy ones, summer. We grill, we have a picnic, we use ketchup and eat hot dogs and as a result, they will and almost always go on sale and a coupon comes out making them dirt cheap! Cough drops and soup are another easy giveaway! When do we get sick? Winter! We have to stay inside and it's cold. Both of these products go on sale and usually have coupons making them very cheap. Evaporated milk usually goes on sale during the holidays because many recipes call for them. As you start to pay more attention, you will start to see the trends!

My suggestion: start small. Don't immediately begin tracking every item on your list or you will slowly go crazy and walk away from couponing all together. Start with a few key items from the "need" portion of your list. Then, once you have a good grasp on those, you can expand your tracking list one item at a time.

Also, keep in mind that price tracking is especially important for those items with short expiration dates. These are items that you will be buying more often and ones that you may not always get the chance to pair with a coupon. So knowing your prices and knowing when to buy can save you a ton of cash even when there isn't a coupon in sight.

ROTATE, ROTATE, *ROTATE*

Here's the deal. Even though you buy enough oatmeal to last you a year that probably doesn't mean that you won't buy any more before the year is up.

Let me explain. Let's say that you are 3 months into your year's supply of oatmeal, and you come across another great sale. Well the logical thing to do at that point would be to restock your stockpile up to the level you have decided on. Then, you still have your year's supply and you can wait until you find the next great sale to buy more.

The problem with this approach is that many people just take the new product and load it right onto the front of their shelves. If you do this long enough, you will eventually come across a box of something that is older than several of your children. Not something that you particularly want to eat!

Luckily there is an easy fix for this problem. It's all about the rotation! When you bring in a new product, make sure that you take the time to clean out your shelf and put the oldest product first and the newest product last. Then you are always pulling from the oldest part of your supply and keeping the items turned over. It a practice that does take some time, but it greatly cuts down on waste and will save you tons of cash in the long run.

USE YOUR FREEZER

So many people are surprised to find out that I freeze cheese. I buy many perishable items that most would assume are only good for a few weeks and freeze them. Cheese, cooked eggs, juice, candy all go into my freezer along with normal items. Learn to use your freezer; it's an asset in the stockpile game.

SET A BUDGET

The entire stockpiling concept is built on saving money! Almost every week I spend around the same amount of money on groceries, and my stockpile grows! Some weeks I spend a little more, some a little less. BUT building a stockpile should NOT negatively affect your budget. If soup is on sale for $.25 per can, I check the expiration date, estimate how many I will use and buy appropriately. I don't go out and say, "I want 500 cans because it's cheap!" Be practical!! Don't spend your entire grocery budget on stockpiling two items that you won't use all that often. Another important stockpiling tip, buy the free stuff in mass! If it's free, stock up. If soup is free, buy as many as you can! If you don't use it all, give it away to friends, neighbors or the food bank! Important thing to remember, don't ever clear a shelf when stockpiling. Stores and other customers get upset when this occurs, I live by a simple principle: be kind, leave some behind!

HOW MUCH IS TOO MUCH?

When you find an item that is free or extremely cheap when using a coupon, the inevitable question arises, how much should I buy? To begin, you need to figure out how large of a supply you need! We recommend having at least a minimum of 3 months on hand, but 6-12 months is preferable. This will allow you to take that item off your grocery list for an extended period of time. Sales are cyclical, which means that eventually that item that you are purchasing today, will *probably* go on sale down the road again. I say probably because there is no guarantee and it's best to stock up while you can. How much of a particular item you need depends on your family and their usage. A family with 4 teenagers is going to use a lot more deodorant than a family with a newborn and a toddler. Determine how much your family needs by estimating how much they use in a given week or month.

THE RIGHT PRICE FOR YOU

Some stockpilers hate paying for anything! Sometimes that leads to small problems down the road. For example,

I hate paying for macaroni and cheese. I rarely have a supply of it because I can't ever seem to get it entirely free. Luckily we don't eat it much, but when I want it, sometimes I have to run and pay full price for one box at the convenient store (A horrible thing). What is the lesson here? Find the right price for you.

BRAND LOYALTY AND STOCKPILING

Brand loyalty is another issue when stockpiling. Most couponers have thrown brand loyalty out the door, but some people only use Dawn. If you find that item on sale and you have a coupon, it may be worth overbuying by normal standards if you know it's the **only** brand that you will use and it doesn't often go on sale.

Now I know that this is a lot of information. It can be a lot to take in and it represents a major lifestyle change for many individuals. But keep in mind that the idea here is to make this system work for you and for your family. This may mean that you only stockpile one to two items at a time or it may mean that you go all out and soon find yourselves storing toilet paper under your kids' beds.

Either option is fine!

It's not about having a carbon copy of what has worked for someone else. It is about finding the right mix to make the system work for you. When you find that perfect balance you will be amazed at the money you are able to save as well as the peace of mind that comes from knowing that no matter what, a lost job or a turbulent economy, your family will *always* have food on the shelves.

WE USE COUPONS. YOU SHOULD TOO!

Chapter Seven
Grocery Psychology

Have you ever wondered about end caps? You know, those nice wide shelves that grace the end of each and every aisle no matter what store you find yourself walking through on any given day? I used to think that those were the *"special"* shelves. The places where stores put all the best deals and the first place I should look if I was looking for something new and wonderful.

It turns out I was half right on this one. End caps, as I have learned, are nothing more than billboards that hold product. They represent a single facet of large scale marketing efforts that most of us aren't even aware of. I'm telling you, now that I know what to look for, I often feel like I spend my day dancing through the advertising version of Swan Lake with each move and cue choreographed to perfection.

And that is exactly what we are going to talk about in this chapter.

We are going to switch gears for a bit as we pull back the curtain and gain a better understanding of the other side of the coin. What do I mean by that? Well, I mean that we are going to dig deeper into the psychology of a sale and find out why stores operate the way that they do.

THE PSYCHOLOGY OF A SALE

Now, before we jump in with both feet here, the first thing we need to understand is the psychology of the sale itself. Think that sales are designed to give us good deals on the products we know and love?

Not a chance.

I mean, it's a nice thought, but it's simply not true. The truth is that a sale is just another form of advertising. It is a marketing technique that stores use, **rather successfully I might add**, to get you and me to walk through their doors each and every week.

Often called *"Loss Leaders"* within the retail industry, stores slash their profit margins on sale items in hopes that you will fill your cart with non-sale products that make up the difference.

Let me give you a quick example. Say that Coca-Cola products are on sale at Bi-Lo this week 4 for $10. That's a great price. It's a price that snags my attention and one that would have most hardcore soda drinkers heading to Bi-Lo this week to stock up.

Here's the thing. When you go to Bi-Lo are you going to **just** buy your Cokes? Or are you going to go ahead and pick up anything else you might need while you're there? Yep, you're going to fill your cart with the milk your kids pour on their morning cereal, add a loaf of bread or two to make lunches and even possibly pick up some meat for dinner.

The Coke sale got you in the door, but your weekly shopping habits took over from there. Sneaky, huh?

WHY DO CERTAIN ITEMS GO ON SALE?

Okay, now that we understand *what* a sale is, (a creative way to get you inside the store) it's time to move on to *why* specific items go on sale.

To understand this we must first understand that a grocery store, well honestly *any* kind of store, is really a business within a business. They are the middleman and therefore are doing business on two fronts each and every day.

The first face, the public one, is what you and I see each and every time we walk through the door. This is the wide shiny aisles, the clean orderly shelves and the impressive weekly sales that keep us coming back for more.

The second face is the B2B or business-to-business side of the house. This is the haggling with vendors, checking product upon delivery and corporate deals that none of us ever get the chance to be a part of. And, believe it or not, this is where the sales come from.

They don't come from consumer demand or requests; they come from corporate deals, trends and special incentives.

Need an example? Let's go back to the Coke sale we were just talking about. Did you know that Bi-Lo was most likely *not* the company that initiated that sale? Nope, Coke did. Maybe a holiday was coming up, or maybe they had a new can design they wanted to début, the reason doesn't really matter. What matters is that Coke came to Bi-Lo with an offer: Buy X-amount of our product for this sale and we will offer you this great low price point that you can't get any other way.

This, my friends, is a sale and it is the type of deal that happens every single day in every single store.

Let me jump in here and say that this is **not** a bad thing. It's not! I am pointing this out so you can understand the system that stores use and get a peek inside their heads. The hope is that if you understand the process then you can take steps to make it work for you and your needs.

How?

Well, for starters, don't fall into their trap!

If you go into a store for a certain item, then walk out with that and that alone. Don't give in to the impulse buy and don't pay more for something you know you can get cheaper somewhere else. Understand what a sale is and use it for your benefit. **Remember, shop smarter, not harder!**

SALE CYCLES

Now that we understand where sales come from, the next thing is to try and predict them. How do you do this? Simple, you time them.

Here's the deal. Every company has a marketing strategy for their products. They know when they want to do a "push," (fancy marketing word for ramping up the advertising efforts) and they know it well in advance. Trust me when I say these are not spur of the moment decisions. In fact, the ads you and I see every day were planned and created months, even up to a year, in advance.

If you start to track the prices on your favorite items, you will begin to see trends emerge. Before long you'll learn to recognize both highs and the lows as well as start to anticipate when a sale should be showing up. And while the cycle length varies from company to company and product to product I have found that a three month cycle is pretty standard in the grocery industry.

I'll be upfront and tell you that this isn't something you'll be able to do right out of the box as a brand new couponer – that is unless you have older more seasoned friends who are willing to share their secrets. So just keep your eyes open. You'll be amazed at how quickly you learn to recognize that rock bottom price you're looking for.

PRODUCT PLACEMENT

This one's huge. Have you ever taken a step back and really **looked** at a grocery store shelf? Not just the one right in front of you, but the whole shelf from top to bottom.

It's kind of impressive.

See, there's a science to how grocery stores are set up and every factor is taken into account. Everything from how the aisles are ordered to how products are packaged, right on down to where each item sits on the shelves is considered and weighed before a final decision is made.

Why does this matter? Because where a product sits both in the store and on the shelf has everything to do with advertising and very little to do with price point. A sale is one thing, we all understand that one, but product placement is something completely different.

Want to know how a product gets featured on the highly coveted end cap? They pay for it! Ever walked into a store and found a huge display of some new candy or drink that you just saw advertised on TV or even in a magazine? That's not an accident! And have you noticed that all the "best" brands have their products stationed right at eye level while you have to squat down to find the cheap version? Yep, they pay for that, too!

You need to know that all the good spots come with a price, one that companies are more than willing to pay. It's a business within a business and once you understand the game you can play it to your own advantage.

Here are a few good examples for you to think about:

SHELF SPACE

Why are all the best products at eye level? Because that is where we naturally look! See, companies know that the average shopper is lazy. I don't mean this as a bad thing, but it's true and we are! We are pretty spoiled in that we don't like to look for things and will generally grab the first thing we see that fits what we are looking for. That's why those eye level spots are so coveted!

The next time you go to the grocery store, realize that there is more than one set of "eye level" going on as you walk through the store. If you look down about 2 shelves, especially on the cereal and snack aisles, you'll notice that the colors get brighter and the packages get a lot more fun. Yep, grocery stores aren't just marketing to you, they are also marketing to your kids. So what is placed at just the right height for little hands? Why, all their favorite things, of course!

I know, for instance, that goldfish crackers are **always** on the low shelves. A fact I am reminded of every single time I head to the store with a set of little hands.

END CAPS

We have already touched on this a bit, but I want to point out that end caps are very much like revolving billboards. They change every week, sometimes even more often, and they reach a staggering number of people on a daily basis.

What's the difference between an end cap and a billboard? You can't buy off a billboard. It's sneaky advertising, but it's still advertising and it works!

SPECIAL DISPLAYS

Have you ever seen the large freestanding displays that get parked in the middle of aisle or out in the open at the front of a store?

You guessed it, advertising. Stuff is everywhere you look!

These types of displays are usually reserved for a seasonal product, special sales or product launches and they are stationed in what the stores refer to as their "action alley." Action alley is the retail space located between the outside wall and the goody packed inner aisles. It's an area that sees quite a bit of traffic and one that can turn product quickly.

One good thing about these types of displays is that they are a great spot to find high value manufacturer coupons. So even the product isn't on your list, take a minute to check for coupons to use at a later date.

HOW MARKETING EFFECTS YOUR SHOPPING HABITS

So stores are crafty. They have this marketing thing down to a science and they have trained us to shop the way they want us to.

Don't believe me? Well, think about your local grocery stores. Think about every grocery store that you are likely to visit in a given month. Chances are good that they each have a similar set-up and that's not by accident. It's because research has proven that we as consumers are hard wired to shop in a certain way and the stores want to capitalize on these in-grained habits.

Let's think about this for example: Have you ever wondered why milk is usually in the back of the store? There is a simple reason. Almost every customer that comes in the door needs milk. So, in order to get it, the store makes them walk by every product imaginable. The hope is that you will be tempted to buy something else besides milk.

Another shared trick by marketers of the years is to convince consumers that bigger sizes are a value, then pull a bait and switch. For years, consumers have been trained to call larger size products, 'value size products'. While often the unit price of these products can be cheaper, these products more often than not are more expensive by unit. You are now paying for convenience.

Let me quickly explain why this 'value size' isn't really a value. The basic principal of buying smaller is this: you can only use one coupon per item. If the coupon specifies a specific size, then you must use it on that size product. If the coupon states "any sized product," then you've just hit jackpot. Trial sizes are your friend! Which would you choose: 4 trial size deodorants you pay $0.00 for or 1 full size deodorant you pay $2.00 for? The answer should be obvious. Smaller items are generally cheaper and using a coupon on every single item you buy drives the unit price way down. Always look for smaller sizes. Ignore the marketers and the 'value size' products. You'll be surprised to find that many of the smaller sized products will be free if you use a coupon!

Beyond that, I want you to realize that marketing campaigns are designed to hit you on all fronts. More so, they can do it without you ever really realizing what's happening. First, you see a commercial. You watch it, partly because the volume on your TV rises slightly when it starts and partly because it makes you smile, but you don't really register what it's for. Next, you see a print ad, or two, or seven, the number doesn't matter. What matters is that each time you see the logo it makes an impression on your mind whether you mean for it to or not.

Then you go to the store. "Oh look! They are sampling something. Let's go see what it is…Oh! A new kind of granola bar. I've wanted to try this!" (Have you really? Or have you just seen it dangled in front of your face enough times that you **think** you should try it?)

This is the effect of marketing my friends and I promise that it has influenced what you put in your cart more than you might think.

IN CONCLUSION...

My goal with this chapter has been to help you recognize marketing and advertising for what they are and to free yourself from this trap. Once you know the tactics, they are easier to avoid. And, once you find the strength to say "No!" you will get control of your grocery budget like never before.

I'm giving you all the tools, but it's up to you to take control. Use their methods against them and save money. By knowing what game they are playing, you can play too!

Chapter Eight

Ask for Help... Then Ask Again

Did you know that couponing is a highly fluctuating process? Believe it or not, it absolutely is! Literally, just when you think you have everything figured out you'll turn around and find a whole new set of policies staring you in the face.

It's frustrating. I get that. But it's not the end of the world. And the best way to navigate all the twist and turns that are inherent to the couponing world is to learn to *ask for help*. It can be hard to do, especially for you beginners out there, but once you get the hang of it, I promise that this one little habit will make your life infinitely easier.

So in this chapter we are going to learn to ask for help. Not just *how* to ask the questions, although that's important, but also **who** to ask and what questions really matter.

Let's get started!

WHY SHOULD YOU ASK FOR HELP?

Because this is generally not a process you can do on your own. Unless you want to make couponing your complete and full time job there is just no way to keep up with all the details that are floating around out there.

The coupons, the sales, the policies, the special incentives, the list goes on and on and it's just far more than one person can manage.

The beauty is that you don't have to manage this by yourself. Help is out there in the form of other couponers, store personnel and even an endless stream of tips and tricks floating around on the Internet. (Not to mention this book.) Help *is* out there. All you have to do is take advantage of it.

WHO SHOULD YOU ASK?

Now, I realize that not all of you are going to be comfortable walking up to a stranger in the store and asking for help. I get that. It's an option, but I get it. So, instead of focusing on just one person to ask, I'm going to give you a quick list. It's not all-inclusive, but it's a good start and its meant to get you thinking.

COUPON WEBSITES

Okay, shameless plug here: Ever been to WeUseCoupons. com? If not then I hope you'll stop by soon. We have tons of real time information about all your favorite stores. Most of the information is contributed by your fellow couponers. Here's the deal- if you need help, register and read. If you have additional questions, simply ask! Within a few minutes someone will respond with help! Coupon forums and blogs are a powerful place to find information and seek help from friendly faces. They are your biggest and best asset.

OTHER COUPONERS

Once you get over your fear of them, other couponers are, for the most part, an amazing resource! Not only do they understand what you are going through, but they know the language and they probably know what you are looking for. Plus all of them have probably been in the position of needing help themselves a time or two.

So just ask them!

If you see that big binder propped open in the cart, just walk up and sweetly ask for some help. If you know couponers in your church or at work, talk to them! Who knows, you might find out about sale you didn't know about, or you could even have a coupon to spare that your fellow couponer would love to have.

STORE PERSONNEL

They might not always be friendly, but store personnel are usually a great asset to help you. Yes, we've all heard the horror stories about the evil cashier that seems to make it her own personal mission to make your life hard, but for the most part store employees are a great source of information. They can get you rain checks, give you a coupon policy or clear up a confusing point about it, check inventory levels, and point you in the right direction almost every single time.

YOUR FAMILY

Ask your family? You might think I'm crazy, but I mean it. You could ask them to help you clip or sort your coupons. You could ask them what they think about different items that are on sale, such as will they eat or use it! Ask them for their extra coupons! You could also ask them for storage ideas. My point here is that your family should be a great source of support for you. So use them, and if they are not supportive, bribe them with a few freebies you got last week! That should make them change their tune a little!

WHEN SHOULD YOU ASK?

When should you ask for help? Any time you need it. This isn't a time to think back and go "Man! I wish I had _____." With so many resources at your disposal you should always take the time to ask for clarification any time you might need some help.

Plus, this whole process is about saving money. It's about gaining control of your finances like never before. And if you don't know what you are doing then you won't be able to maximize your savings. So suck it up and ask for help when you need it.

WHAT SHOULD YOU ASK?

This is a grey area. What I mean by that is there are questions to ask…and there are questions to stay away from depending on the person you are talking to.

For example, your store manager isn't going to appreciate you asking "Why are you always out of everything I want?" That's not going to make them happy and it's not going to make them want to help you.

However, if you were to ask, "What is your policy on rain checks?" or "Do you have any coupons today?" then they are likely to be quite helpful. Especially if you ask in a polite way.

Keep in mind that different questions should be asked to different people. So, you can ask whatever you want, just make sure you ask the right person.

- Do you have a coupon policy?
- Does your store double?
- When do your new sales start?
- Do you accept coupons?
- Do you have a coupon limit?
- Does your store offer rainchecks if a product is out of stock?
- Where is your clearance section?

Questions are important, and learning to ask the right questions to the right people can make your entire couponing experience more positive. I've solved more problems with a smile than I ever did with a frown. So, as hard as it can be to walk up to a stranger with a smile on your face, I challenge you to do just that. I promise it's worth it and I promise it gets easier every single time. Before you know it, you will be the person standing there with a smile on your face and you will show some new couponer the ropes.

WE USE COUPONS, YOU SHOULD TOO!

Chapter Nine

Giving Back

The thing about coupons is that they have opened my eyes to a whole new way of life. Not just because of what they can do for my own family, but for what they allow me to do for others.

Let me explain.

Before I started couponing, my wife and I would see a person or family in need and we would **wish** that we could help them. I mean, sure, we might be able to spare a small amount of money every now and then, but there was no way we could make a true and lasting difference in anyone's life.

It was heartbreaking and it's a feeling that I'm sure many of you are more than familiar with.

Enter the coupon again.

From day one, right from that very first trip to the store when I scored free shampoo, I knew I was on to something big.

From that day forward my life was going to change…..and I was **right**. Coupons have literally opened my eyes to a whole new world in so many ways and I can't even begin to explain the opportunities they have offered my family.

For starters, I can share my knowledge. I can use every forum available to me to share what I have learned with others that it might help. This book. My website. Coupon classes. FrugalTV on YouTube. My Social Media Outlets. The forum may vary, but the message is the same on every front.

But also, I now have the opportunity to give back like never before. Not in money, but in goods and in food and in the items that people need when things get hard. In fact, this year my wife and I have a goal to give an equal amount to what we make.

That is huge for us! I think that it would be huge for anyone.

And it doesn't stop there. Now instead of hearing about a person in need and wishing that I could do more, I know that I can make a difference. That I can feed that person and that I can share with them the skills I have used to change my financial future.

It may sound far-fetched, but I'm not alone. I hear stories from couponers all over the country telling me how they have used their skills to make a difference in their own communities.

I'd like to take a minute to share a quick story with you. This comes from my good friend Lynn and I am very thankful that she was willing to let me share her tale with you.

Lynn lives in the south, and I won't tell you where, I will tell you that it is one of the very same areas devastated by a day of deadly storms in early 2011. When I called Lynn to check on her after the dust had settled, she had a story to tell me that I really didn't expect.

The first thing Lynn did on that stormy Wednesday morning, as she does almost every Wednesday morning, was to head out on her weekly grocery run. No, she's not coupon crazy, she just had no idea that the weather forecast was quite as crazy as it ended up being.

Turns out that this was a HUGE week for Lynn and she ended up walking out with almost $800 worth of items for just under $90. She was ecstatic because although she regularly saves around 50% she had never had a trip even close to this one.

The only problem was the items that she ended up buying weren't ones that she had a great need for. When I asked her about this, she didn't really have an answer. Maybe she was distracted by the storms, or maybe she was excited about the savings, but either way Lynn had a car full of toiletries and groceries she had no idea what to do with.

Fast-forward 24 hours. Lynn is home, watching the news, and understanding for the first time the extent of the devastation that has hit her hometown. Then a list flashes up on the screen. It's a simple list of items outlining what the shelters desperately need in order to help those left homeless by one tornado after another.

Why did that matter? Because Lynn had almost every single item on that list still packed in the back of her car. The items they needed were the exact items she bought at the grocery store the day before without a clear understanding of what she would do with them. She didn't even unload them.

The answer was simple. Before the news even ended Lynn was in her car driving to the closest drop off point to unload her items. She never once questioned it, just knew that it was meant to be.

Why do I tell you this? Because you never know when you may have the opportunity to help someone in need. Lynn couldn't have offered hundreds or thousands of dollars to the relief effort, but she could drop off almost a thousand dollars worth of goods without breaking her bank or devastating her budget.

So now I pass the challenge on to you. I challenge you to find your own opportunity to give as you use your new skills to help those around you. It won't be hard to find, just keep your eyes open and be willing.

WAYS TO GIVE

The opportunity to give is all around us. So much so that it can be hard to know where to start or where your donation will have the most impact. I'll be the first to tell you that I don't have all the answers, especially to this type of extremely personal question. But I can give you a place to start.

Here are a few ideas to help you get the ball rolling.

FOOD BANKS

Food banks can always use donations. And, while they will take just about anything, they always have a wish list. So give them a call and keep on top of what they are looking for. Then you can keep an eye out as you do your weekly shopping.

WOMEN'S SHELTERS

The thing with women's shelters is that the people that go there often walk through the door with nothing more than the clothes on their backs. Not only the women, but also the children that often come with them. So if you know of a local women's shelter than I am sure that they could use some help. Again, the best way to find out what their needs are is to give them a call. Find out what they are looking for and then see how you can help.

CHURCH

If you belong to a church, then they will generally offer you endless ways to help. Not only do many churches operate their own food pantry, but they also have connections with local nonprofits that need help. Think of it like a one stop shop. You can go to one place and learn several different ways to help those around you.

MILITARY CARE PACKAGES

This is a cause that is near and dear to my own heart. In fact, one of my appearances on *Extreme Couponing* was dedicated to sending a large number of care packages to our troops stationed overseas. These men and women risk their lives daily for each and every one of us and the least that we can do is show our appreciation in some small way. Care packages are a great way to do this. I can promise that something as simple as a fresh toothbrush, a pack of baby wipes and a box of tea bags is very appreciated by those who deserve it the most.

YOUR OWN BACKYARD

The reality is that you never know when you're going to come across someone who needs a boost. So be ready. One of the things that I picked up from my friend Beth is to keep a giving box packed and ready to go. She takes a medium sized cardboard box packed with goodies at all times. Then when she hears about a family or person in need she just snatches it up and hands it over. It has led to some pretty powerful moments for Beth and her family and it is a great experience for her to offer her children.

SCHOOLS

You would be surprised that schools are always in need of health and beauty supplies. From wipes to deodorant, school resource centers help needy kids. I personally work with a local elementary school and deodorant for their puberty lessons. Next time you drop your kids off, ask the principal if they accept donations.

The bottom line is that we are surrounded each and every day by endless opportunities to give. So do it. Take the time to give back to your community and share the bounty with those in need. We've all been there. We've all had hard times, and we know what it's like to need a hand. I promise it's worth it and once you do it the first time you'll be hooked.

I know I am.

WE MADE IT!

And that's it. We have officially reached the end of our journey, and I hope you have enjoyed yourself as much as I have.

I also hope I have taught you more than a thing or two along the way.

We use coupons, you should too. That's my challenge for you. Sharpen your new skills. Don't let couponing intimidate you. I know that there are plenty of details, and it can appear complicated. Trust me, if **I** can do it, **you** can too!

Still have questions? You know where to find me! Anytime you're feeling overwhelmed, just head over to WeUseCoupons. com and you'll have all the answers you could ever need. Our forums are packed with friendly faces and helpful tips, our blog is up and constantly updated and you can even email me directing if you still can't find the answer you need.

You didn't think I'd abandon you now, did you? Of course not!

Now, good luck and **Happy Couponing**!

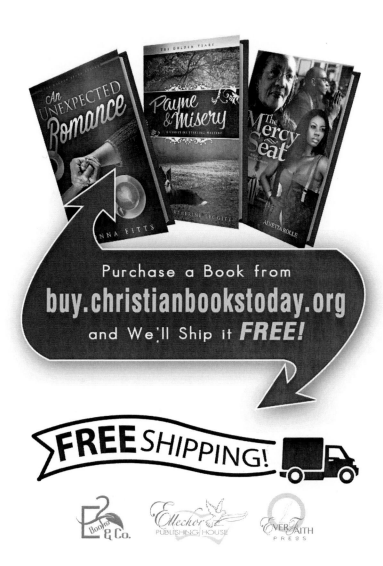